INTRODUCTION TO LAPIDARY

ROCK TUMBLING
CABOCHON CUTTING
FACETING
GEM CARVING
AND OTHER SPECIAL TECHNIQUES

CHILTON BOOK COMPANY

Radnor, Pennsylvania

INTRODUCTION TO LAPIDARY

PANSY D. KRAUS, G.G., F.G.A.

Published in Radnor, Pennsylvania 19089, by Chilton Book Company

Designed by Adrianne Onderdonk Dudden
On the cover: Three fine-faceted andalusites, each averaging
8 carats, with rough specimen. Photograph, Laura J. Ramsey.

Manufactured in the United States of America

Library of Congress Cataloging in Publication Data
Kraus, Pansy D.
Introduction to lapidary.
Suggested Reading: p 188
Includes index.
1. Gem cutting. I. Title.
TS752.5.K73 1987 736'.2'028 86-47958
ISBN 0-8019-7266-3 (pbk.)

5 6 7 8 9 0 6 5

CONTENTS

PART TWO: CABOCHONS

PART THREE: SPECIAL LAPIDARY TECHNIQUES

PREFACE

INTRODUCTION TO LAPIDARY is intended as a basic guide for the amateur lapidary and hobbyist, presenting the different types of gem cutting and polishing, from tumbled stones, cabochons, and bead making to lapping, sphere making, gem carving, mosaics and intarsias, and faceting. Rather than providing extensive technical information on each of these forms of lapidary work, this guide describes the basic processes and techniques and provides helpful hints for the hobbyist.

Each lapidary technique is highlighted by the work and the methods used by amateur and professional lapidaries who have won prizes for their art works and gems. Each artist began as a hobbyist, and the examples of their work are meant to inspire you by showing just how far you can advance once you select the lapidary hobby that appeals to you most.

Separate chapters on lapidary equipment feature the latest, most technologically advanced units and tools on the market. These chapters are also intended as a guide to introduce you to the equipment available. Equipment can be obtained from a local dealer or from catalogs advertised in the many lapidary magazines and journals included in the References at the back of the book. The Suggested Reading list is extensive and will lead you to the best references for obtaining more information on the hobby you choose.

If you are fortunate enough to live in an area where you can find a lapidary instructor or can join a local gem and mineral club, you will be one step ahead. Even if you must learn on your own by trial and error, this book offers you a solid foundation and will lead you to explore advanced lapidary techniques and whet your appetite and open your imagination to the many possibilities for becoming a creative lapidary artist on your own.

ACKNOWLEDGMENTS

I wish to express my thanks and appreciation to all of my friends and associates who have helped in so many ways in order that this book could be completed.

I wish to thank all those persons who have contributed photographs and information: Harold and Erica Van Pelt Photographers for the historical photographs of Idar-Oberstein; Dale T. Blankenship; Olive M. Colhour; A. D. Daegling, Jr.; William R. Dindinger; William E. Grundke; Bernard N. Kronberg; Hing Wa Lee; Warren Bowen; Claire Curran; Maurice G. "Maury" Maline; Earl Manor; Jerry Muchna; William Munz; Betty Phetteplace; Laura J. Ramsey; Bob Jones; Mary Warzin; and Joe H. Borden.

My thanks and appreciation to the following manufacturers and suppliers for providing photographs and information about their latest equipment and supplies: ARG Sales Company, Inc.; Covington Engineering Corporation; Crystalite Corporation; Diamond Pacific Tool Corporation; Estwing Manufacturing Company; Fran-Tom Lapidary Equipment, Division of Contempo Enterprises; Gryphon Corporation; Norman T. Jarvi Company; Geo-Sonics, Division of Geode Industries, Inc.; Imahashi Manufacturing Company Ltd.; Lortone, Incorporated; M D R Manufacturing Company, Incorporated; MK Diamond Products, Inc.; Contempo Lapidary; Mohave Industries, Inc.; Ultra Tec; Raytech Industries, Inc.; and The Rock Farm.

I wish to express my thanks to Dara E. Yost and Gerd E. F. Stittel for the line drawings, and to Harry H. Waugh, Jr., a friend of many years, for his help in obtaining metric conversions; to Jackie Daegling for typing the first draft, and to Virginia A. Englebright and Marjorie Hunn for typing and proofing the final manuscript; to June Culp Zeitner, Special Assistant Editor for *Lapidary*

Journal, for her constant encouragement and advice throughout the project; and to Willard Woolfolk, Lapidary School Director, and his instructors of the San Diego Mineral and Gem Society for their cooperation in helping me to obtain action photographs.

My thanks and appreciation also to all those club members who so graciously took the time and effort to answer numerous questions.

1

HISTORY OF LAPIDARY

The craft of lapidary can be traced back to Early Man, when he first began to clothe himself and fashion his own weapons. Probably his first weapons were rocks that he sharpened by chipping the edges to form a spear point. The spear heads could be lashed to long poles and used for hunting. Smaller, rounded rocks could be chipped on one side only to form a sharpened tool for scraping animal skins and using them as clothing. He made hammers or clubs by lashing rounded or elongated rocks to the end of a short, heavy stick or tree branch.

Man was also attracted to shiny pebbles, which he could use as decorative objects by tying vine tendrils around them and hang around his neck or tie around his wrists and ankles. Witch doctors often ground stones into powder, used as medication or good-luck omens, which was probably the beginning of the many superstitions, legends, and lore of gemstones.

Some of the earliest records indicate that the first forms of gem cutting and carving or engraving were the ancient seals made from the joint of a reed, such as a bamboo, or the curved surface of a conch-like shell, used by the Babylonians and Assyrians and similar to the Egyptians' scarabs, which date back to 4800 B.C. or earlier. The ancient Egyptians fashioned jewels and jewelry from lapis lazuli, turquoise, and amethyst.

From about 500 B.C. to the third or fourth century A.D., Babylonian and Assyrian craftsmen cut circles with a hollow drill made from bamboo embedded with sapphire (corundum) dust.

Fig. 1-1 The large sandstone wheels in the early lapidary shops of Idar-Oberstein, Germany, were powered by water from the Nahe River Canal.

The tenth and eleventh centuries in Europe saw a gradual transition from engraving and cabochon cutting to faceting.

In 1290, a guild of gem cutters and polishers was formed in Paris, and a century later diamond cutting and polishing was being carried on in Nuremberg, Germany, although the procedures and methods used were not known. Subsequent to that date, the "Tablecutters" of Nuremberg joined with the stone engravers to form a guild that allowed young men to become apprentices. An apprentice was bound to serve five or six years under a master lapidary before he was considered skilled enough to set up his own shop.

At the beginning of the fourteenth century, cabochons were the main decorative feature in the German, Austrian, and Russian crowns.

In 1407, diamond-cutting techniques improved under a gem cutter named Hermann. In 1456 in Bruges, Belgium, Louis de Berquem, a long-time resident of Paris, announced that he had discovered a method of diamond cutting. Ten years later, his contemporaries and peers considered him the "father of diamond cutting."

During the Renaissance, carving and engraving flourished and even sur-

Fig. 1-2 The artisan-craftsmen of Idar-Oberstein working the old sandstone wheels in a lapidary shop in the nineteenth century.

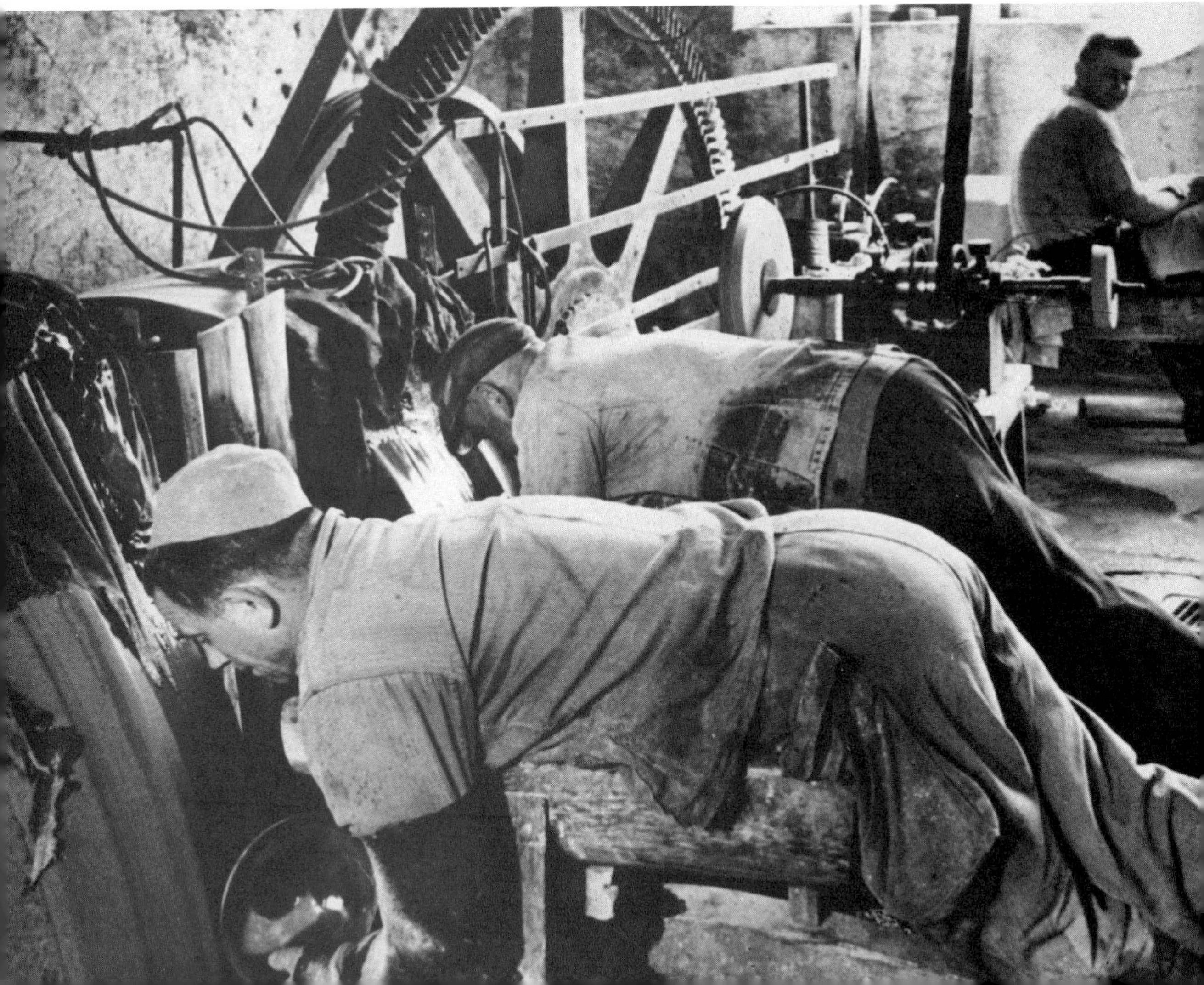

Fig. 1-3 The Gebruden Leyser cutting shop is today one of the largest shops in Idar-Oberstein. The cutter in the center is the grandfather of the family. Note the dop pot to the left of center and the wheels on the right. Photograph by G. Presser. Courtesy, Harold and Erica Van Pelt Photographers.

passed the work of the early masters. The early forms of gem cutting were mostly cut en cabochon, that is, cut with a flat bottom and a rounded top. This form of cutting is still used today.

Diamond cutting flourished in France until the French Revolution, when many cutters fled from Paris to Amsterdam, Antwerp, and Lisbon, where they continued their trades. About this same time in England, lapidaries were unsurpassed in the working of colored gemstones, and Idar-Oberstein became the ornamental and colored gemstone cutting and carving center of Germany (now West Germany) and remains so today.

In the United States, there was little activity in the field of lapidary until the 1930s, when European craftsmen emigrated to New York to serve the jewelry industry. With little information available, some of the earliest American lapidaries persevered in their craft and began a correspondence with each other to exchange information, since few references or tools were available. George Frederick Kunz, a collector of gemstones and carvings and a buyer for museums, published one of the first books on lapidary.

In 1933 the late H. C. Dake started the *Mineralogist Magazine,* and Peter Zodac started *Rocks and Minerals Magazine*, which is still being published. These two men attempted to keep the channels open to other amateur lapidaries, such as James Harry Howard and L. E. Bowser, a machinist, who started to build their own lapidary equipment by trial and error. Through these four men, lapidary methods were introduced to other amateur gem cutters.

In 1935, J. Harry Howard compiled all the available information into his book entitled *Handbook for the Amateur Lapidary*. The demand for the book was so great that Howard had to revise and update it to include the latest improvements and techniques. In 1946 he published the *Revised Lapidary Handbook*, which contained diagrams and instructions for building lapidary equipment and gave instructions on faceting and cutting and polishing cabochons.

In 1937, the magazine *Mineral Notes and News* was started in the Southwest, later to be renamed *Gems and Minerals*; it catered to the lapidary and jewelry-making hobbyist until it ceased publication in 1986. Then in 1947, Lelande Quick founded *The Lapidary Journal* for the lapidary, jewelry maker, and collector. The number of lapidaries and collectors of gems and minerals continue to grow, and today many journals and reference books are available on every form of lapidary.

PART ONE

TUMBLED ROCKS

2

ROCK TUMBLING

Tumbling is perhaps the oldest form of grinding and polishing stones, beginning not with lapidaries but with nature itself through the slow process of erosion. Tumbling gemstones is a slow process, just like nature's, and it requires patience.

Tumbling actually developed from cabochon cutting and faceting. The small pieces of stones that were left over from the pieces that were being cut could be polished in a baroque (irregular) form and used in jewelry or in making mosaics.

SELECTING THE ROUGH MATERIAL

The stones most often tumbled by the amateur lapidary are agate, jasper, petrified wood, flint, or other similarly massive stones. You can collect stones on field trips, swap with friends or club members, or purchase them from dealers who advertise in gem and mineral magazines.

Rocks should be sorted according to hardness. If you try to tumble hard and soft rock together, the softer rock will pulverize before the harder rock starts to show a polish. Rocks are segregated according to Mohs' scale of hardness, which is a comparison scale rather than an actual hardness scale. Mohs' scale of hardness simply means that one rock is harder or softer than another rock. For example, quartz, which is 7 in hardness on Moh's scale, will scratch

Fig. 2-1 A group of tumbled gemstones: agates, jaspers, rhodonite, rhodochrosite, turritella agate, petrified wood, carnelian, and amethyst.

orthoclase (feldspar), which is 6 in hardness, but it will not scratch topaz, which is 8 in hardness.

Another hardness scale, the Knoop scale, was formulated by a twentieth-century chemist from a series of indentation tests, using a diamond point as the indentation tool (see the Appendix). In addition to these two scales of hardness, a third scale has been devised by the U.S. Bureau of Standards. Mohs' scale of hardness is the one most often used for gems and minerals:

Mohs' Scale of Hardness

Talc	1
Gypsum	2
Calcite	3
Fluorite	4
Apatite	5
Orthoclase	6
Quartz	7
Topaz	8
Corundum (natural)	9
Diamond	10

PREPARING THE STONES

Tumbling gemstones involves four major steps: (1) rough grinding, (2) medium grinding, (3) fine grinding, and (4) polishing. Lapidaries who produce finely polished tumbled stones often divide the polishing step into two steps. After the fine grinding, they prepolish before the final polishing.

All stones should be sorted by approximate hardness. Some stones even of the same hardness may be brittle. Sort out and save the brittle stones until you have enough for a complete batch to tumble separately. (Obsidian and Apache tears should always be tumbled separately. Although both are forms of volcanic glass, they react differently in the tumbler.)

The stones should be about ½ inch (12.7 mm) to 1½ inches (38.1 mm) at the widest or longest dimension. Larger rocks will have to be broken so that you will have enough to fill the tumbler. To break the rock, you will need a stone mason's hammer or crack hammer, a chisel, and a heavy steel plate. Place the steel plate on several thicknesses of newspaper or similar padding on a sturdy surface. The padding under the steel plate will absorb some of the shock of the blow. Wear safety goggles or safety glasses and a strong pair of protective gloves, preferably leather gloves with a small gauntlet to protect your wrists against flying rock.

Fig. 2-2 Bracelet chains are designed for cementing preformed tumbled stones to the pads (top), or connecting capped stones to the chain with jump rings (below).

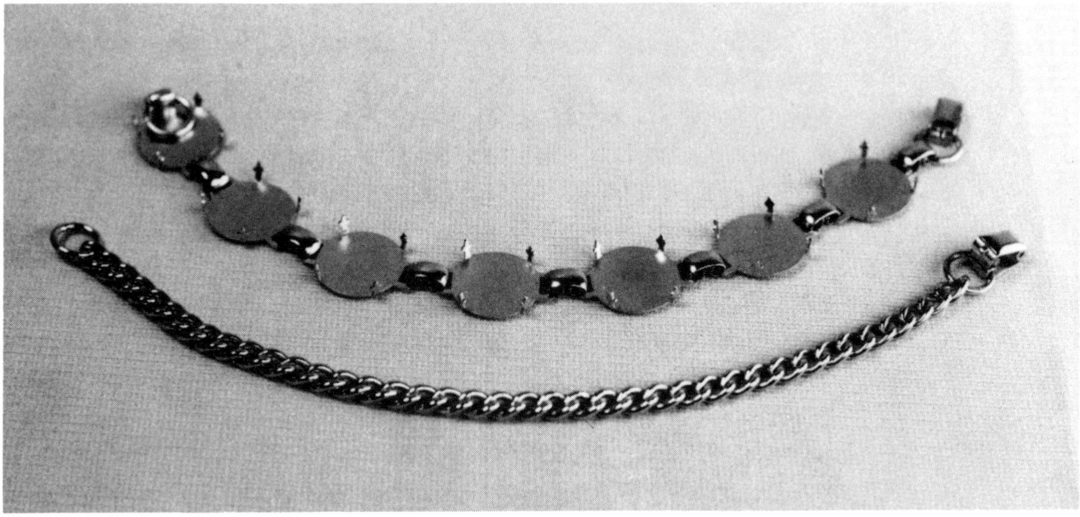

Check the rock over carefully for a fracture line, then place the chisel on the line and give the chisel a quick sharp blow with the hammer. If the rock does not break completely, strike it again, but with a lighter blow to prevent the rock from shattering. Do not allow anyone else to stand close when breaking rock. The chips fly with quite a bit of force and an onlooker could be injured. Anyone standing near should also wear safety goggles or safety glasses.

If you are just learning tumbling, start with chalcedony, agates, jaspers, flint, or chert. These gemstones, all varieties of cryptocrystalline quartz, are 6½ to 7 in hardness and are the least difficult to work with. They are tough enough to withstand most of the problems the inexperienced hobbyist may encounter in tumbling the first few batches of stone.

Wash all cracked or hammered stones thoroughly. For stubborn dirt, use a stiff brush, such as a vegetable brush. Dirt cuts the grinding action of the abrasive. Examine them for internal fractures or concave areas that cannot be eliminated in the coarse grind. Set aside any stones with such fractures or concave areas. You may be able to break the rock again and use it in the next batch. Any stones that are pitted or have a spongy matrix will not polish well, so discard them. Also discard all the slivers and small chips. The crystalline areas of chalcedony can be polished in the same way as lace agate, but put them to one side until you have gained more experience.

Make up a log or record sheet so that you will have an accurate record of every stage in the tumbling process, as well as the amounts of items used and the operating time in the tumbler. The log sheet will come in handy the next time you tumble similar stones.

Use an average of ¾ cup (206.478 ml) to 1 cup (275.304 ml) of abrasive for each 8 to 10 pounds (3.6287 to 4.5359 kg) of rock. Too much abrasive will slow down the grinding process and make the slurry too thick. If you do not use enough, the abrasive will break down before the batch is finished. Add ½ teaspoon (2.8677 ml) to 1 teaspoon (5.7355 ml) of baking soda to the stone and abrasive, depending upon the instructions you are following.

THE ROUGH GRIND

If you are using a medium-size tumbler, fill the tumbler approximately ⅔ to ⅝ full. The tumbler *must* be at least half full. Then take the stones out of the tumbler and weigh them and calculate the proper amount of abrasive for the weight. Put the stones back in the tumbler and add the abrasive. For 8 to 10 pounds (3.6287 to 4.5359 kg) of rock, use ¾ cup (206.478 ml) to 1 cup (275.304 ml) of abrasive. For the rough grind, use either 1F grit or 80 grit abrasive. (Most advanced hobbyists recommend the 80 grit.) Shake the abrasive down in between the stones and add the baking soda to help prevent gas build-up. If the rocks in a batch are about the same size, you will have to use a filler to carry the abrasive in between the gemstones; otherwise, the stones will not be ground down uniformly. Then add enough water to almost cover the rock. The water should be just visible but should not cover the top layer of the rock completely. Put the lid on the barrel and seal it tight. Then start the tumbler. At first you will hear a clicking sound. After about 24 hours, turn off the tumbler and check the progress.

Within two or three days, the clicking noise should quiet down and become like a rumbling swishing sound. This is when most of the grinding takes place in the rough-grind step. The average load (a few larger stones and the rest medium to smaller stones) should take approximately 6 to 7 days. Some hobbyists advise opening the barrel every day or two to relieve the gas build-up and to check the load.

If you must turn off the tumbler for several hours or more after the grinding operation has started, empty the tumbler and clean the stones, as you will have to start the run again with new abrasive. The abrasive and stones will dry into a hard mass and the tumbler will be difficult to clean. Pour all tumbling waste into a container with a wide opening. When the liquid has evaporated, break it up and discard it. Never dispose of tumbling waste by pouring them down plumbing drains. When the tumbling waste dries, it hardens like cement and is difficult to remove. Carefully pour or lift the stones into a plastic colander or pan and wash them thoroughly and carefully.

Never use metal utensils. Metal will mark the stones, and the only way to remove the marks is to regrind the stones. If the process is still in the coarse or intermediate grind, it is not as serious since the fine grind will remove the marks, but be careful not to chip the stones.

After washing the stones, inspect them carefully. Set aside any stones that have been chipped or are pitted and not completely rough-ground and retumble them with the next batch of rough stones. If many stones are pitted or chipped, put the entire batch back through another rough grind before continuing. Any stones that have bad fractures on the surface will have to be rebroken and started with a new batch of stones.

The stones must be completely clean and free of any grit from the previous grind. Any coarse grit that is carried into the intermediate grind will scratch the stones and the intermediate grind may not remove them. Let the stones dry and check them again; wet stones are deceptive and you may not see the cracks.

THE INTERMEDIATE GRIND

When stones are ready for the intermediate grind, they will have a frosted appearance when dry and should not show any jagged or sharp rough edges. If you do not have enough stones to fill the tumbler to the proper level, you will have to use a filler and additives: ¼ teaspoon (1.4338 ml) of baking soda and ½ teaspoon (2.8677 ml) of detergent. If the load is only half full, use 1 cup (275.304 ml) of filler, such as plastic tumbling pellets. Also use 1 cup (275.304 ml) of either 3F or 400 grit abrasive. Add all dry ingredients first; then add enough water to cover the top layer of stones only halfway. Proportions given here are for approximately 10 pounds (4.5359 kg) of rock.

The tumbler should run 6 to 7 days. After the first 24 hours, you can open the tumbler to inspect the stones and release the gas. Check the consistency of the slurry; if it looks too thick, you may have to add some water.

Most experienced hobbyists use a double-barrel tumbler and prepare enough stones to start two coarse grinds at the same time. If you start two coarse batches at the same time, you should have more stones that you can use in one intermediate grind. Save the extra stones and tumble them with the next intermediate-grind batch. Store the stones in plastic or cardboard containers and label them so you can identify them quickly. Whenever you combine two different lots, be sure the stones are the same type and hardness.

When the intermediate grind is finished, wash all the stones and the tumbler thoroughly so that no grit is carried into the fine-grinding step. If you have used tumbling pellets, wash them thoroughly and save them for reuse. Sort the stones carefully, laying aside any that are cracked or chipped. If any stones have deep chips, you may have to put them through another rough grind. If the scratches are fairly shallow, you can put them into the next intermediate grind.

THE FINE GRIND

Fine-grinding is the next step. Handle all the stones carefully and put them gently into the tumbler. For the fine grind, use 600-grit abrasive. If the tumbler is not two-thirds full, add plastic tumbling pellets to bring the load to the proper level. Use ¾ cup to 1 cup (206.478 ml to 275.304 ml) of filler; then add ¼ teaspoon (1.4338 ml) of baking soda and 1 to 1½ teaspoons (5.7255 to 8.6032 ml) of detergent. If the stones are at a ⅔ to ⅝ level in the tumbling drum, pellets will not be necessary.

The fine grind takes about 7 days. You can stop the tumbler after 24 hours for inspection; then reseal and start the tumbler again.

After the third day, stop the tumbler and take out several stones to see if they will take a polish. You can do this easily if you have a lapidary polishing wheel or polishing buff. Otherwise you can use a piece of heavy felt or a piece of untreated leather, using the hide side.

Place the stone on a solid surface; apply wet polish and rub the stone briskly back and forth. If the polishing agent begins to dry out, add a few drops of water. Rub the stone energetically with a firm, but not hard, pressure. Stones that have been ground enough to take a polish should start to shine in a few minutes. If the stones will not take the polish, then you will have to tumble them again in the 600 grit.

Return the stones to the tumbler and continue the fine grind.

POLISHING

To prepare for the polishing step, wash and sort the stones and check for pits or spalling (fine chipping or flaking on the edges of the stones). Lay aside any stones with pitting or spalling and retumble them in a fine grind with another batch. Chipped or lightly flaked stones will not polish well. Any stones with rough edges or pits will scratch the good stones in the polishing step and ruin the whole batch.

Place the good stones in the tumbler. For 8 pounds (3.6287 kg) of rock, add ½ cup (137.652 ml) of tin oxide; for 10 pounds (4.5359 kg) of rock, add 12 to 14 ounces (340.194 to 396.983 gr) of polish. Then add 1 cup (275.304 ml) of soap flakes, 1½ cups (412.957 ml) of granulated sugar, and enough tumbling pellets to bring the barrel load to at least ½ to ⅝ full. Replace the lid on the tumbler, seal it, and start the tumbler. Check the stones every 24 hours. They

Fig. 2-3 A bracelet and a pair of dangle earrings made from capped tumbled stones. Stones were selected by size and color, then capped and connected to the chain with jump rings.

should look the same whether wet or dry. The polishing takes from 3 to 4 days.

BURNISHING SOFT STONES

Once you have become experienced with agates, jaspers, flints, or cherts, try some of the softer gemstones. Soft stones will usually need a burnishing stage. Wash all stones gently and thoroughly and put them in the clean tumbler. Add 1 cup (275.304 ml) of soap flakes for each 4 pounds (1.841 kg) of stones, and ¼ cup (68.826 ml) of granulated sugar. After the stones have been burnished, place them carefully in plastic containers. Burnishing is helpful in removing polish from crystallized pockets if you have been tumbling feldspars or lace agates or agates with crystallized areas.

TUMBLING PREFORMS

Preforms are stones that have been cut to an approximate shape on a diamond trim saw and ground to shape on the coarse silicon-carbide wheel of a cabochon unit. The stones need only a short time in the rough-grinding step to remove the saw marks and deep wheel marks.

The preforms—and gemstones that you tumble with preforms— should always be the same type and hardness. A small tumbler works well with preforms.

Prepare a tumbler load of stones of the same material for regular baroques. After the rough grind, the original load will have decreased by about 20 percent. Before starting the intermediate grind, add the amount of preformed cabochons necessary to bring the tumbler content back to its regular ⅔ level. Then add ½ cup (137.652 ml) of coarse abrasive used in the original grind and restart the tumbler. Check the progress every day. As soon as the saw marks and deep wheel marks have disappeared from the preforms, stop the tumbler. Prepare the intermediate grind and continue with the standard tumbling procedure.

If you are tumbling a large group of small preformed cabochons (for example, stones that are under 16 by 18 mm), you do not have to tumble them with baroques. They can be tumbled by themselves because they are small enough to mix properly in the barrel without additional baroques to carry the grit in between them. Preforms will not have the sharply defined edges of a

Fig. 2-4 To cap stones, press them into Styrofoam to hold them upright while the cement dries. Caps should be shaped to the stone before cementing.

regular cabochon since the tumbling rounds off all the edges. This type of cabochon is usually used for cementing into inexpensive jewelry mountings.

TUMBLING SMALL SLABS

The maximum diameter of small slabs should not be over 2½ inches (63.5 mm). The slabs do not have to be the same size or of the same material, but they must be the same approximate hardness.

The main difference in polishing small slabs is that the tumbler must be loaded in layers. Place a single layer of slabs in the tumbler, then cover that layer completely with the small stones that you will finish as regular baroques. Repeat the layering process until you have enough stones for a batch of baroques. Each time you change the abrasive, you will have to layer the slabs and the small stones. The amount of slabs in any one batch should not be over 20 percent.

Small slabs can be tumbled with a softer material, but adapt the tumbling process to the softer material, not to the slabs. When you inspect and sort the stones, be sure to remove any chipped stones, whether baroques or slabs, so they will not scratch the other stones in the batch.

For polishing to be successful with small slabs, you must have enough baroques to act as buffering and carrying agents to tumble against the slabs. A good carrying agent for agate slabs is Apache tears. Do not worry about the polish on the Apache tears; you can wash them and save them for another batch. Using a softer carrying agent will ensure that the slabs will not become scratched.

When polishing slices of a crystal-lined geode, the solid band of agate around the outside should be an unbroken circle. Since a partial slab exposes the crystallized area, it will continue to crack, and small pieces will break off and scratch other pieces in the tumbler.

When transferring from the coarse grit to successively finer grits, be sure to remove all of the coarse grit from the crystal centers. A few grains of coarse grit can easily become lodged in the crystal cavities and will dislodge into the finer grit and scratch the other slabs. When tumbling larger slabs, tumble only one at a time. (Slabs that are large enough for clock faces require much larger tumblers than will be discussed here. Before trying to polish the larger slabs, you will need more experience.)

DESIGNING WITH TUMBLED STONES

Tumbled stones can be used in a variety of projects, from gem trees and inexpensive jewelry items to decorative floral arrangements. They can also be used to make mosaics, tabletops, designs in garden or patio walks, and in fireplace fronts. One hobbyist uses her tumbled stones to create landscape "paintings" (see color Fig. 12). Using only the tiniest pieces, she sorts the stones into various colors. After sketching a light outline of the landscape on an artists's canvas, she cements the stones to the canvas to form the landscape. The cement must be one of the quickset cements that will dry transparent. The canvas is then ready to frame and hang as a work of art.

The most popular use of tumbled stones is inexpensive jewelry, and you do not need any jewelry-making skills. All you need are the stones you have tumbled and some small caps, which you can purchase from your lapidary supplier or rock shop or from a lapidary supply catalog. The caps are flexible and can be shaped to the stone before applying the cement. You will need a good cement that will dry clear (some hobbyists recommend Epoxy 330) and a

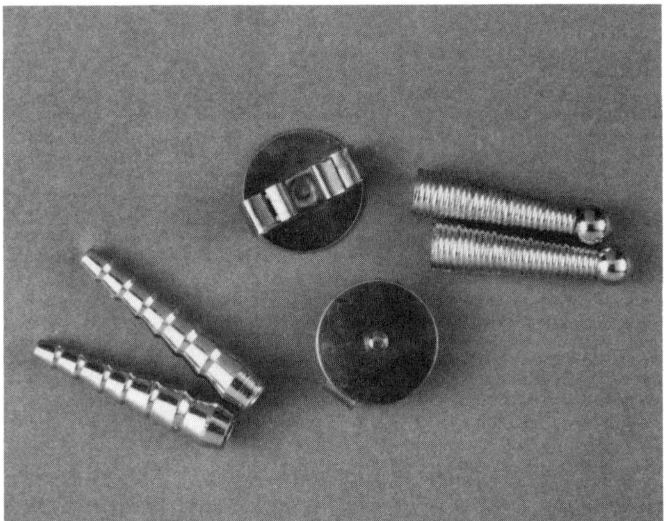

Fig. 2-5 Two pairs of bola tie tips in different styles; in the center is the tie slide, to which a tumbled stone or a cabochon can be cemented, and the back of the bola slide, showing the loops that hold the cord.

Fig. 2-6 A special tumbled stone attached to a key chain makes an attractive accessory item.

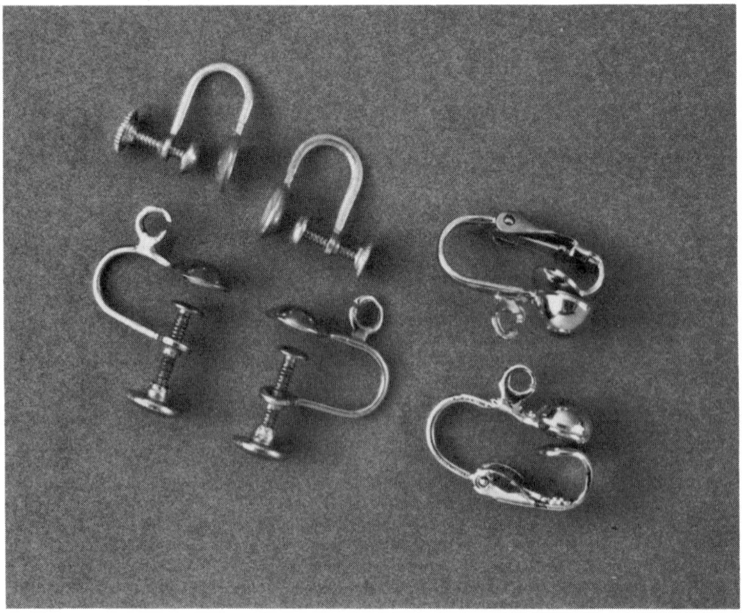

Fig. 2-7 Clip-on and screw-on earring findings.

block of Styrofoam for holding the stone and cap upright until the cement is thoroughly dry.

Be sure to clean both the cap and the stone with denatured alcohol or acetone to remove any fingerprints or dirt on the stone. Fingerprints will leave a thin oily film that will prevent the cement from adhering to the stone. Press the stone into the Styrofoam block, form the cap to the stone, apply the cement, and set it back into the Styrofoam. Allow the cement to dry according to the directions on the label. The capped stones can be used on a neck chain, a key chain, a bracelet, or on the ends of a bola cord.

Two pairs of jeweler's pliers work well for attaching capped stones to neck chains, bracelet chains, or key chains. Use the pliers to close the jump ring that joins the stone to the chain. The most commonly used pliers are a pair of chain-nose pliers and a pair of flat-nose pliers. If you are attaching only one stone to a neck chain, you can use a locket loop. You can obtain the necessary items from a lapidary supply shop or from lapidary catalogs.

If you have chosen a mounting that has been designed especially for tumbled stones, you do not need to cement a cap to the stone. Most mountings designed for tumbled stones have flat pads to hold the stones. Select the flattest side of the baroque and cement it to the mounting. Some mountings have small prongs or loop bezels that can be pressed against the stone after the cement is dry, using a burnishing tool or stone-setting pliers.

Gem trees have become popular with tumbling hobbyists, and several booklets are available with instructions and a list of the items necessary to make the trees. Tree kits are also available and contain all of the supplies needed, together with instructions.

Fig. 2-8 Studs and wires for making pierced earrings.

3

EQUIPMENT FOR ROCK TUMBLING

Until lapidary equipment manufacturers started building tumblers, lapidary hobbyists had to experiment and improvise their own. Some manufacturers now specialize in building only tumblers, much to the delight of amateurs and professionals alike.

There are two major types of tumblers—the horizontal or rotary tumbler and the more recent vibrating tumbler. The rotary tumbler is the most popular, probably because it is less expensive. Before you invest in a tumbling unit, decide how you will use it. If you are a faceter or want to make cabochons and wish to remove only the outer skin of the rock so you can better select the perfect stone, then a small tumbler will be ideal. If you want to make jewelry, gem trees, or mosaics, a medium-size tumbler will be more efficient because you can tumble larger quantities of stones.

The smaller tumblers, those of the pint (550.61 ml) and quart (1101.22 ml) sizes, are not as sturdily built as the 2¼-quart (2477.74 ml) size or larger and will not work as efficiently for as long a period of time as the larger, sturdy tumblers.

ROTARY TUMBLERS

A rotary tumbler is shaped like a barrel or cylinder and is either round, six-sided, or twelve-sided, and it has a tight-fitting lid that clamps on (Fig. 3-1). The

Fig. 3-1 A small rotary tumbler is perfect for tumbling small quantities of gemstones. Courtesy, Lortone, Inc.

Fig. 3-2 Many hobbyists prefer the convenience of a hexagonal-shaped barrel with a rubber liner. Courtesy, Contempo Lapidary.

barrel rotates continuously in one direction on a pair of parallel shafts. The tumbler must be watertight to prevent the water and abrasive from leaking or spewing all over the workshop. The abrasive used in the tumbling process is referred to as loose grit or loose abrasive. The loose abrasive or grit is suspended in water as the barrel revolves. When the proper mixture of water and abrasive is obtained for the best grinding condition, it is referred to as "slurry." Some authorities say that the stones will not begin to be ground until the slurry has been obtained.

Most experienced or professional tumblers recommend a hexagonal barrel with a heavy rubber or plastic liner (Fig. 3-2). A heavy rubber liner is easier to seal and less gas builds up in the barrel. Tumbling is a continuous process once the tumbler has been started. Time estimates for tumbling are based on a continuous running time from one to several weeks for each grinding process. Tumblers are designed to run twenty-four hours a day for several days or weeks.

Small Tumblers

Some of the smaller inexpensive tumblers have a plastic barrel with a rubber liner and a jar-type lid. These tumblers tend to have a short life span. Abrasives work their way into the threads of the lid and under the seal and make it impossible to keep clean—a prerequisite in all lapidary work. The thick, all-rubber-lined barrels are much better in terms of durability and efficiency. The shafts are operated by a continuous-run motor that does not usually overheat. Some smaller units have fan-cooled motors that have proven to be reliable and efficient.

Many small tumblers have a rubber "O" ring instead of a standard V-belt that connects the drive shaft and the motor. The "O" ring gradually stretches causing the drive shaft to slip, and eventually it will break. The standard V-belt with pulley is more reliable.

Some small tumblers have plastic barrels and drive shafts mounted in plastic bearings. The plastic-sealed bearings are not supposed to need lubrication, but some experienced hobbyists lubricate them with a few drops of lightweight machine oil after running several batches of stones continuously because the bearings run more freely.

Often the barrel shafts are covered by plastic or rubber to increase the friction. With use, the shafts will develop shiny or smooth spots and begin to slip. These spots are usually the result of abrasive or slurry leaking or being

Fig. 3-3 A medium-size triple-barrel tumbler will let you tumble two batches of stones in the rough grind and one in the intermediate grind, or any combination of rough, medium or fine grind. Courtesy, Covington Engineering Corp.

Fig. 3-4 A tumbler mounted at an angle makes it easy to check the progress of the grinding, release the gas build-up or add water if necessary.
Courtesy, Covington Engineering Corp.

spilled on the shafts. When slippage begins to occur, the plastic may have to be lightly sanded.

Medium-Size Tumblers

A medium-size tumbler is the best size for the average hobbyist. Medium-size tumblers have a capacity of 6 to 12 pounds (2.72 to 5.4431 kg.) Three-barrel tumblers (Fig. 3-3) have a capacity of 75 pounds (34.0194 kg), with each barrel having a capacity of 25 pounds (11.3398 kg) of rock.

THE TUMBLING BARREL

The interior of the tumbler barrel may be round, hexagonal (six sided), or decagonal (ten sided). Most small tumblers have round interiors, although many hobbyists who have medium-size tumblers prefer the hexagon-shaped barrels. The shape of the barrel interior determines the tumbling speed. A round barrel requires higher RPMs (revolutions per minute) to overcome the amount of slide or slippage of the contents being tumbled. If the RPMs are too slow, the rocks will slide down the side of the barrel and not tumble at all. If the RPMs are too fast, the stones will cascade too high on the inside of the barrel before being thrown from the sides. When this happens, the stones will chip or crack each other.

The hexagonal-barrel requires a much slower RPM for the polishing step. The recommended speed for the polishing step is 25 RPMs, and the tumblers are set for that speed. The grinding steps run at the same speed, so they take longer than the polishing step. Some of the larger tumbling barrels that are not rubber lined are subject to greater gas build-up. Every experienced hobbyist has an opinion as to what causes gas build-up in the barrel. Some have attributed it to fermentation of living organisms that cling to the rock and to the chemical breakdown of the silicon carbide in the grit when combined with water. Other hobbyists think it is directly related to the temperature of the workshop. Gas can be controlled by thoroughly cleaning the rock before starting the tumbling process, operating the tumbler in the coolest area of your workshop, and opening the tumbler for daily inspection. Never let the tumbler run longer than two or three days without checking it. Inspecting the tumbler every day is the best way to alleviate the gas build-up which can cause the tumbler to explode.

SELECTING A TUMBLER

Before purchasing a tumbler, consider how you will use it. If you concentrate on tumbling rather than on the other forms of lapidary, select a medium-size multiple-barrel unit. If you use the tumbler as a supplementary piece of equipment, a small tumbler with an extra barrel will be all you will need.

Some manufacturers make a beginner's tumbling kit with a small tumbler (some have a double-barrel unit), a book of instructions, and all the necessary abrasives for one batch of stones. Some kits even include the stones. If you decide to continue to tumble stones and purchase a medium-size tumbler, keep the small unit. You will always be able to use it for tumbling small amounts of special stones or for preparing stones for faceting or making cabochons.

BUILDING YOUR OWN TUMBLER

If you are a build-it-yourself person, try to attend some gem and mineral shows where dealers demonstrate tumbling equipment. Talk to the dealers and ask questions about how the tumblers are constructed and how they operate. You might want to purchase a small tumbling unit and try it for a while to see if you like tumbling before building your own unit. (See Suggested Reading for books and articles on building rock tumblers.)

A word of warning: If you decide to make your own tumbler, do not use a glass container for the tumbling barrel. The glass will grind away as fast as the rock, if not faster. Glass is about 5½ to 6 on Mohs' scale of hardness, which ranges from 1 to 10. Many of the stones that you will tumble will probably be 6 or more in hardness. The glass barrel will wear thin quickly and will shatter. Anyone standing close could be cut and you will have stones and slurry all over your workshop.

VIBRATING TUMBLERS

Vibrating tumblers are a comparatively new form of lapidary equipment. These innovative tumblers are comprised of a drum or multiple drums mounted upright on a vibrating plate. The barrel is positioned on four heavy springs on the plate; underneath is a double end shaft with a small pulley on each end. The drive belt from each pulley is connected to another shaft that has an ec-

Fig. 3-5 An upright vibrating tumbler allows you to check the contents, add water and release the gas without turning off the motor. Courtesy, Geo-Sonics Division of Geode Industries.

centric mechanism that creates the vibrating action. The vibrating action can be increased or decreased by changing the weight on the shaft.

The manufacturers recommend that vibrating tumblers be opened and checked every 8 to 10 hours. The slurry thickens readily and will have to be thinned out more frequently than in a rotary unit. But, unlike a rotary tumbler, you do not have to turn off a vibrating tumbler. You can add water while the tumbler is operating because the barrel is upright and has an opening at the top. The water should be added very slowly, and only enough water should be added to allow the stones to move around freely.

Cleanliness is even more important with a vibrating tumbler than with a rotary tumbler, and it is often harder to maintain. The barrels are much more difficult to clean. Hobbyists who use vibrating tumblers recommend a separate barrel for each grinding stage when tumbling certain stones, such as Apache tears. Unfortunately, the barrels are expensive, as is the unit itself.

A vibrating tumbler will do some things that a rotary tumbler will not do,

Fig. 3-6 Some vibrating tumblers are designed to operate with a dry compound instead of slurry. Tumbled and mounted stones can be burnished at the same time. Courtesy, ARG Sales Company, Inc.

such as polishing stones set in rings. This can be done in a dry compound with other cabochons tumbling at the same time.

ABRASIVES

The silicon-carbide abrasives used for tumbling, available at lapidary supply stores and rock shops, are graded by number. The higher the number, the finer the grit. The first abrasives used in lapidary work were inorganic—quartz (flint), garnet, corundum, emery (a mixture of aluminum oxide and iron oxide), and diamond. Garnet, corundum, and diamond are still in use today. Since the turn of the century, man-made abrasives primarily silicon carbide, have become popular because they are efficient and economical.

When silicon carbide is manufactured, it is first broken into 1-inch (25.4 mm) chunks and then rolled and crushed into grains. It is passed over screens of a given mesh size and graded according to the size of the mesh. For example, 100 grit means the abrasive has been passed over a mesh screen that has 147 particles to one linear inch. The finer grains, from 240 and higher, are graded by a sedimentation or centrifugal separation process.

The most common grit sizes used in tumbling are the straight-graded 80, 100, 220, 320, 400, and 600 grits (see the table of grit sizes in the Appendix). The 600 grit is often considered a prepolish abrasive. Some hobbyists use an F-graded abrasive for the rough and intermediate grinds and then switch to a standard-graded 600 grit for the fine grind.

The F grading system—1F, 2F, 3F, and 4F—means the grit size is not fully graded. For example, 1F is 280 grit. This means that it contains some finer grit but none coarser than 280; 2F is 320 or finer; 3F is 400 or finer; 4F is 500 or finer. The ungraded grits are usually less expensive. It is not advisable to use an F grade just before going to the polish step.

Hobbyists have tried using reclaimed abrasives made from recrushed silicon-carbide grinding-wheel cores, plus abrasives used for other processes. These are less expensive but do not work as well as pure silicon carbide abrasives because they contain a considerable amount of fillers and bonding agents from the wheels, as well as other impurities.

There is little difference in price between the prepackaged abrasive and loose abrasives sold by the pound (.4535 kg), unless you are going to buy in quantities of ten pounds (4.5359 kg) or more. Prepackaged kits can be purchased in three- or four-step kits. The three-step kits have 100 grit and 600 grit plus the polish. The four-step kit includes the intermediate grind (either 220 or 400), as well as the 100 and 600 grits, and the polish. If you use the three-step kit, the fine-grinding stage will take longer than usual in order to compensate for the missing intermediate grind.

Buying loose abrasives in large quantities is less expensive, but you will need extra storage space. Wherever you store abrasive must be completely dry. Loose abrasives will not deteriorate, but they will absorb moisture, mak-

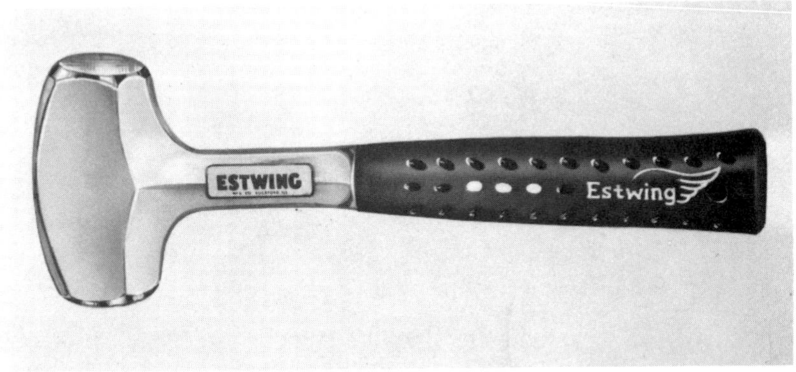

Fig. 3-7 To break rocks into smaller pieces, use a mason's hammer or a crack hammer with a chisel and wear safety goggles. Courtesy, Estwing Manufacturing Co.

ing them more difficult to measure. If your workshop is in a basement or a garage that has a cement floor, store the abrasives on wooden platforms or skids to allow good air circulation. When storing the abrasives on shelves, always put the finest abrasive on the top shelves and the coarse abrasives below. If you should spill fine abrasive into a coarser abrasive, no real damage has been done, but if you spill the coarser abrasive into the fine abrasive, your stones will be scratched during grinding and your fine abrasive *must* be replaced.

FILLERS

Fillers can be used in the various stages in tumbling to help carry the abrasives or polish in between the rocks in the tumbler. They can also be used to thicken the slurry so that the gemstones will not chip when tumbling against each other. When the stones are large and of the same size, plastic tumbling pellets can be used to carry the abrasive between the rocks so they will grind down properly. A filler is also necessary in the polishing step. Plastic pellets may be round, oval, or wedge-shaped. Walnut shells or wood chips can also be used as fillers. In the polishing step, fillers such as wallpaper paste or granulated sugar will thicken the slurry and slow the tumbling action to help prevent chipping. The plastic pellets and walnut shells that float when you wash the stones can be cleaned and used again. The fillers that do not float are difficult to reclaim and often have to be discarded with the abrasive or polish.

Some stones create more gas while tumbling than others, probably because of the chemical content of the different minerals and rocks. Adding baking soda will help control much of the gas build-up. Early hobbyists used fillers such as rice hulls and wood and leather chips, but these created unpleasant odors in the workshop because of their bacterial content. Soap powder can be used in tumblers to act as a wetting agent and to thicken the slurry.

POLISHES

The two most popular lapidary polishes are tin oxide and cerium oxide. Some of the other polishes used in lapidary work have specific uses. Levigated alumina is often used as a prepolish before the final polish. Tripoli is a good polish for corundums (ruby and sapphire). Chrome oxide can be used in the polishing step for jade and malachite. Two other polishes used in lapidary work are jeweler's rouge, used for special stones, and Linde A, used in faceting.

PART TWO

CABOCHONS

4

CABOCHON GRINDING AND POLISHING

A cabochon is a stone that can be fashioned into any shape–round, oval, square, heart shape, the shape of a cross, or a free-form shape. The top of the stone is curved into a dome and the bottom is usually flat. Some heart and cross shapes have low-domed tops, whereas others are double cabochons, with each side having a low dome. Sometimes the top of a double cabochon will be much higher than the bottom. Cross shapes are often polished as flats, with the sides at a 90°-angle to the flat top and bottom. Double cabochons and flat stones such as crosses or hearts are usually polished on the top and bottom. The bottom of simple cabochons are often fine sanded.

PREPARING THE STONE

Most slabs of gem material are cut approximately $^3/_{16}$ to $^1/_4$ inch (4.7625 to 6.35 mm) thick. Decide what pattern or shape you want to cut and mark the shape of the stone on the slab with a template and scribe. A template is a thin sheet of plastic or metal with various cut-out shapes. The plastic template in Fig. 4.3 is a popular one with hobbyists because it includes a variety of shapes and patterns. Most templates are marked in millimeters to correspond to the sizes of commercial mountings. You can make a marking stylus or scribe to trace around the inside of the shape on the template from either brass or aluminum

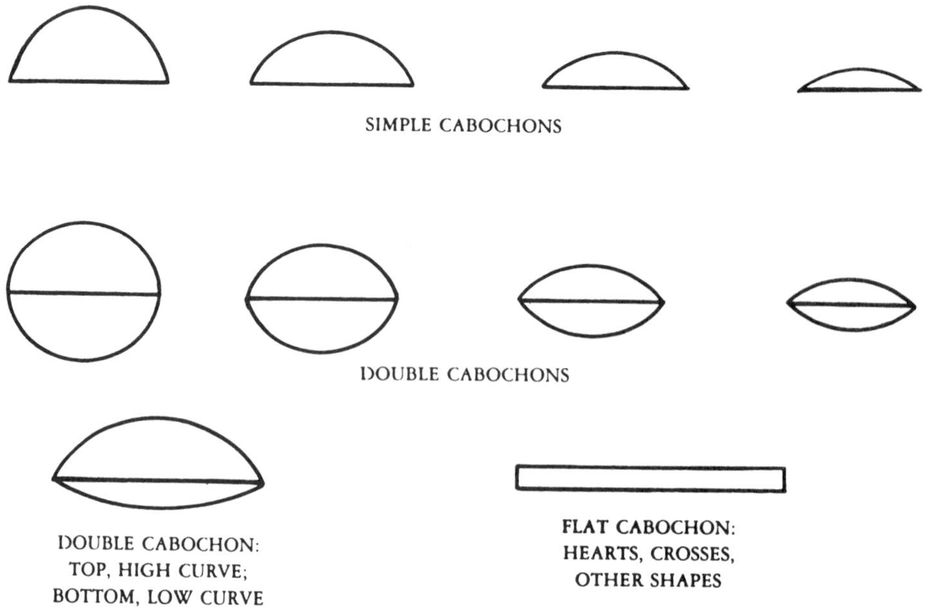

Fig. 4-1 Side views of the "standard" types of cabochons. There is an almost limitless number of free-form shapes. Illustration by Dara E. Yost.

Fig. 4-2 Top and side views of a healed fracture. The side view shows how to place the cabochons in order to use as much of the stone as possible. Illustration by Dara E. Yost.

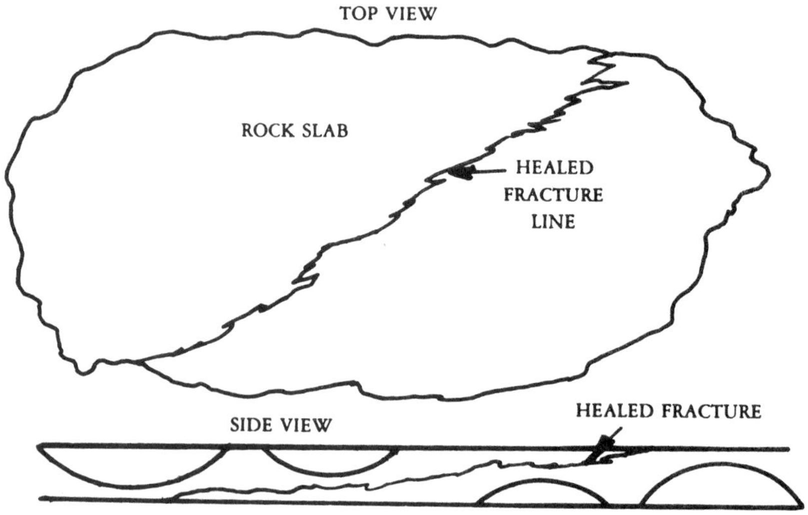

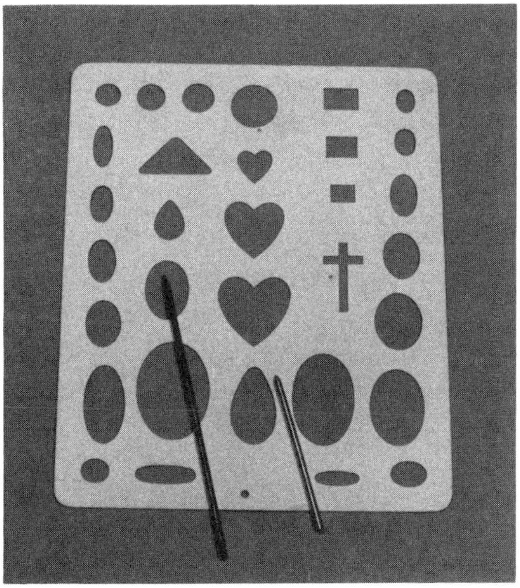

Fig. 4-3 Plastic template and two marking styluses. The longer stylus on the left is a piece of brass welding rod with a sharpened point. The stylus on the right is aluminum welding rod.

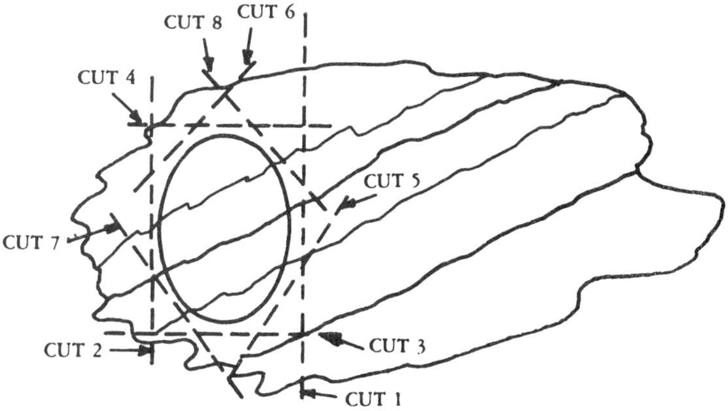

Fig. 4-4 Trim saw cuts made before the grinding process. Any corners left can be ground off on the coarse grinding wheel before dopping the stone. Illustration by Dara E. Yost.

welding rod, cut to 6 to 8 inches (15.24 to 20.32 cm) in length, and grind one end to a sharp point.

After marking the slab, trim it close to the pattern lines with a trim saw, using all straight cuts (see Fig. 4.4). Never try to cut a curve with a diamond saw. Do not cut right next to the template line; allow enough space for the grinding, sanding, and polishing. The template line is a guide and should still be visible when the stone is trimmed. After trimming the stone, wash it thoroughly in warm soapy water to remove all the oil and dirt.

DOPPING

The next step is to mount the stone on a dop stick. Dop sticks are usually made from wooden doweling ¼ inch (6.35 mm) to ⅞ inch (22.225 mm) in diameter, depending upon the size of the stone. Choose a size that is comfortable for you to hold. You will need an alcohol lamp, using denatured alcohol as fuel, or a dopping pot to heat the dopping wax and to warm the stone before mounting it on the dop stick. Dopping wax comes in stick form.

You can make your own alcohol lamp stove from a piece of thin sheet metal 3½ to 4 inches (8.89 to 10.16 cm) wide, formed into a "C" shape. The sheet metal should be 12 to 13 inches (30.34 to 33.02 cm) long so that 3½ inches (8.89 cm) can be bent at right angles to the length on both ends. The bottom end forms a base for the alcohol lamp and the top end becomes a platform on which to warm the stone before dopping.

Fig. 4-5 You can make your own dopping stove from a large juice can. Cut the opening just wide enough and high enough to allow the alcohol lamp to slide in and out. The two stones on the left have been ground but not sanded. On the right is a stick of green dopping wax. Photograph by A. D. Daegling, Jr.

Fig. 4-6 An electric dopping pot. Chips of green dop wax are heated in the receptacle. The stone can be kept warm on the top of the stove. Courtesy, M D R Manufacturing Co.

You can also make an alcohol lamp stove from a large empty fruit juice can that holds 46 fluid ounces (1.36 liters). Remove the label and cut an opening in one side wide enough, about 3 inches (7.62 cm), so the alcohol lamp will slide in and out easily. To give extra strength to the can stove, do not cut the opening close to the other end of the can, but leave about 1½ inches (3.81 cm) at the top (see Fig. 4-5).

A dopping pot is an alternate heating method (Fig. 4-6). Some dopping pots use canned heat such as sterno or a chafing-dish candle; other units are electrically powered. If you use a dopping pot, put small bits or pieces of dop wax into the receptacle and heat the wax to a semifluid state. Do not let the wax bubble or burn; if it does, it will not hold the stone firmly.

To warm the stone, hold it in a pair of tweezers and pass it over the flame before putting it on the dop stick with dop wax. You can also keep it warm by placing it on the top of the alcohol lamp stove or dopping pot.

To apply wax to the dop stick using an alcohol lamp, melt the stick of wax over the flame and dab it on the dop stick. If you are using a dopping pot, dip the dop stick into the heated wax and twirl the stick. With either method, repeat this process until you have enough wax on the dop stick to form to the back of the heated stone.

Fig. 4-7 Sanding the back of a cabochon on a coarse-grit grinding wheel to remove saw marks left by the slab saw.

Place the dop stick on the warm stone while the wax is still hot. Hold the stick vertically and center it on the stone. Do not cover the template marks. Wet your fingertips and form the wax against the stone. If the wax is too hot to touch, allow it to cool for a few seconds before forming it against the stone.

Once you have mounted the stone on the dop stick, let it cool to room temperature. Before starting the grinding process, make sure that the stone is securely attached to the dop stick. If it is not, it will fall off the dop stick when you begin the grinding and fly into the drip pan under the wheels. If this happens, stop the wheels before trying to retrieve the stone. Then start the wheels again and let them spin while you clean and redop the stone.

A waterproof apron is essential when working with silicon carbide wheels. A magnifying glass also comes in handy for checking the stone. You might also want to wear a head loupe like those used by jewelers, which can be raised or lowered as necessary. If you do not have running water in your workshop, keep a pan of water with a mild detergent nearby to wash the stone before changing from one sander to another and before going to the polishing wheel or disc. Keep a roll of paper towels or some cloths handy for drying the dop stick and stone. Cleanliness is essential.

ROUGH GRINDING

The initial grinding done with a 100 or 120 grit wheel, will grind all the corners left from the trim saw and give the stone its basic shape, conforming to the template guidelines. Try not to cut too close to the template lines. You do not want to remove too much material at this stage, since more will be removed during the fine-grinding and sanding stages.

If you want a bezel on the stone, grind it on the bottom edge. The angle of the bezel can vary from 10 to 27 percent, depending on how you will use the stone. Some hobbyists cut the bezel angle as much as 45°. Occasionally, you may want a reverse bezel to fit a certain type of mounting (see Fig. 4-8). A reverse bezel is added after you finish the top of the cabochon and remove the dop stick. If you work carefully, you can redop the stone, placing the dop stick on the top of the finished gem, or you can hold the stone while grinding the reverse bezel if it is a large stone.

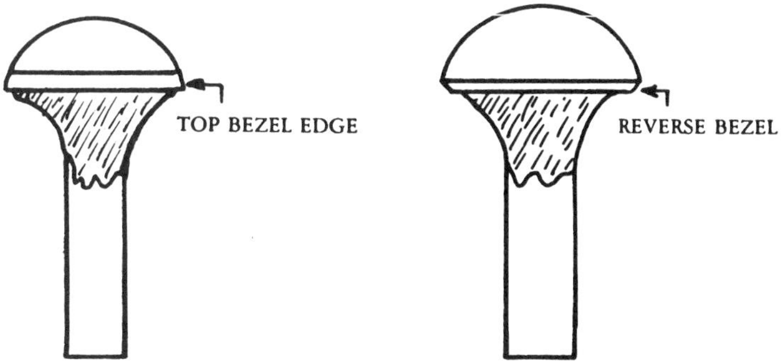

Fig. 4-8 A top bezel can be put on the stone during the initial grinding and sanding. The reverse bezel is usually put on the stone after the top is completely finished and the dop stick has been removed.

FINE GRINDING

The fine-grinding stage, which is accomplished on the fine grit (220 or 230 grit) wheel, will remove all the wheel marks from the rough grinding as well as any deep scratches in the stone. Check the stone carefully as you grind it to be sure you are grinding it symmetrically. When the stone has been evenly ground and is well shaped, it is ready to be sanded.

Always start the initial sanding with the same grit that you used on the last grinding wheel. Most fine-grinding wheels are 220 grit, so the first sanding cloth should also be 220 grit. The sanding can be done either dry or wet. Wet

Fig. 4-9 Dry-sanding a stone with 220 grit sanding cloth after the grinding.

sanding is preferable for most stones and essential for heat-sensitive stones. Durable stones, such as the various agates, can be dry sanded as long as you do not allow too much friction heat to build up. Many hobbyists support the back of the stone with their fingers so they can tell when the stone is getting too warm.

Often the experienced hobbyist will have several stones ready to sand at the same time. The first stone is sanded until the heat begins to build, then laid aside and the next one sanded. In this way you can rotate the stones through the coarse sanding stage, checking to see that all wheel marks and grooves are removed and the stones are symmetrical. The stones are then ready for fine sanding.

FINE SANDING

Wet sanding does not require as much water as the grinding wheels. Some hobbyists simply spray water on a "Wet or Dry" sanding cloth with a spray bottle. As the name implies, "Wet or Dry" sanding cloth can be used either wet or dry. Dry sanding cloth, however, will deteriorate rapidly when wet.

Before fine sanding, wash your hands and the stone thoroughly. Any grit carried over to the fine sanding will cause deep scratches that will not polish out. Start the fine sanding on a 320 or 400 grit cloth. Sand the stone until all scratches are removed and the stone acquires a semigloss or satiny appearance. Stones that are 8 or more in hardness must be sanded on a 600 grit cloth before going to the polishing wheel. If you have not fine sanded, you will have trouble obtaining a good polish on the stone. Wash the stone thoroughly before going to the polishing wheel.

POLISHING

Polishes come in either powder or stick form. The stick form can be applied directly to the polishing wheel or disc. Polishing powders should be mixed with enough water to create the consistency of whipping cream or a little thicker. If the polish gets too thick, it will load the wheel or disc and will not produce a good polish on the stone until some of it is worked off. Apply the polish to the wheel or disc with a 1-inch (25.4 mm) paint brush, then polish the stone to a high shine. Harder gem materials will take a high polish, while softer, more porous stones will have a satiny finish.

Fig. 4-10 Dry-sanding the bezel on a flat-top stone.

Fig. 4-11 Polishing a stone on a leather-covered faceplate with cerium oxide. The faceplate on the other side is for tin oxide.

Polishes

Several polishes can be used, depending upon the gem material being worked. The most common polishes used in lapidary work are tin oxide, cerium oxide, chrome oxide, and Linde A.

Tin oxide is a white polish that is used on a hard felt wheel. It can also be used on a leather faceplate when you use another polish on the hard felt wheel. Tin oxide will polish a wide variety of gemstones.

Cerium oxide, which has a pinkish color, can be used on a hard felt wheel or an end faceplate with either a canvas or leather disc. Cerium oxide, like tin oxide, can be used on many gemstones. Both are standard in most hobbyists' workshops because of their adaptability. Most agates and jaspers will polish equally well with either tin oxide or cerium oxide.

Chrome oxide is green and rather messy to use. It should be used on a leather faceplate that has a guard shield completely around it to prevent the polish from splattering all over the workshop as the polish spins off the faceplate. The hobbyist using it may also acquire a slight greenish cast. Chrome oxide is used to polish malachite, jade, and occasionally rhodonite. When using chrome oxide, always wear a breathing mask.

Linde A is a fine white powder used more frequently by faceters than by cabochon cutters. It is the only polish that can be mixed with another. When polishing cabochons, you can mix one or two parts Linde A to eight or nine parts of another polish to obtain a higher polish. Mix the polishes dry, then add water before applying them to the polishing wheel. Special materials may require special polishes and methods.

Other polishes used in lapidary work are levigated alumina, tripoli, white diamond, and jeweler's rouge, which can be obtained in white, green, red, and black. The last three polishes are most often used as metal polishes, but they also can be used for special gemstones.

Never mix polishes on the same wheel. If you have tin oxide on the hard felt wheel and you need cerium oxide, use the rough side of a leather faceplate for the cerium. If the stone is difficult to polish, use the smooth side of a leather disc.

FINISHING THE STONE

When the stone is polished, heat the wax just enough to soften it and remove it from the dop stick. Then, with a clean sharp knife blade, slice between the stone and the wax and dop stick. If any wax remains on the stone, remove it with denatured alcohol. An alternative method is to warm the wax and twist off the stone, then soak the stone in denatured alcohol to remove the wax.

Before sanding the back of the cabochon, grind smooth any obvious saw marks on the back with the fine grinding wheel. Hobbyists who exhibit in competition often polish both sides of the cabochon. To finish the base, redop the cabochon on the top side in order to have better control of the stone.

DESIGNING CABOCHON SHAPES

Bernard N. Kronberg designs many of his own unusual cabochon shapes, often inspired by gems in the crowns of European royalty or from the heraldic emblems of the early European nations. His designs include a stylized contemporary variation of the French fleur-de-lis, a Cross Crosslet scaled down from the crown of Denmark, and the British Royal Cross on the scepter in the British crown jewels. He has also utilized maple leaves in stylized patterns. See color Figs. 13 and 14 for a number of Bernard's unusual cabochons.

Crosses and other unusual patterns have many curves that cannot be cut on a standard grinding wheel, so Bernard had to be creative and devise other methods of cutting and polishing. When he cuts one of his free-form cabochons, he rough-shapes it on the trim saw by nibbling the inside cuts. To do this, he must make several straight saw cuts close together, cutting into the concave areas that cannot be worked on a grinding wheel. After making these saw cuts, he breaks out the thin strips of material that are left with nipper pliers or wedges a thin strong blade, such as a screwdriver, in between them.

Once he has broken out the thin strips of material, Bernard can get into the curves with small diamond files and sanding-cloth strips made from expandable sanding-drum belts. Another way to get into the tight curves is to use small core drills. Bernard often cuts and shapes his diamond files to fit the area he has to file. He uses the diamond files dry (even though this cuts the life of the files in half) and always with only a very light pressure. Using the files dry leaves a powdered surface that shows the lines of the pattern. If he used the files wet, the water would mask the outline and cover the flat spots and scratches.

Bernard uses only new sanding cloth because worn sanding cloth tends to glaze and will leave scratches. He prefers a low-crowned cabochon top for most of his special shapes because there is a higher degree of reflection than from a high-domed cabochon.

When polishing tight inside curves in free-form agate cabochons, Bernard works by hand, using strips of leather, leather shoestrings, cloth, or paper strips impregnated with diamond paste. He prefers to use strips cut from brown paper bags because the brown paper retains the diamond paste well. He may use bamboo strips impregnated with diamond paste to polish in tiny areas. When Bernard discovers a scratch on a polished surface, he removes all the polish and repolishes the entire area instead of repolishing just the scratch.

CUTTING PHENOMENAL GEMS

Gemstones with special optical qualities are referred to as phenomenal. They may possess adularescence, asterism, aventurescence, cat's-eyes, chatoyance, iridescence, labradorescence, or play of color (opal). Phenomenal gems require special cutting techniques in order to show their special optical effects.

Cat's-eyes and stars in gemstones are the result of the very fine and closely oriented needles or thread-like "inclusions" within the body of the stone. In many instances, the fine, closely packed needles or threads are tubular. If the stone has only one set of needles, when properly oriented, cut, and polished, the result will be a cat's-eye. If the stone has two sets of needles that are straight and closely packed *and* they cross each other, the result will be a four-ray star. Three sets of closely packed needles that all cross each other result in a six-ray star.

For best effect, any star or cat's-eye stone should always be cut as a high-crown cabochon.

Stars (Asterism)

A well-defined needle structure in star stones will be oriented according to the six crystal faces. A cross section of the crystal will have a hexagonal shape if the

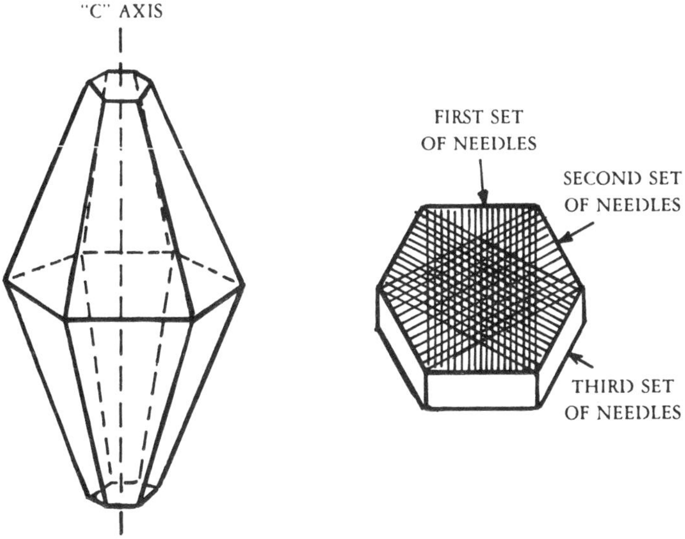

Fig. 4-12 The illustration on the left shows the direction of the "C" axis in corundum (ruby and sapphire). At right is a cross-section taken through the middle of the crystal to show the orientation of the three sets of needles necessary to form a star. Illustration by Dara E. Yost.

outside crystal structure is visible. When cutting a star ruby or sapphire or any other star stone, the base of the cabochon must be at right angles to the "C" axis of the crystal. If any crystal faces show on the rough material, you can determine the "C" axis. The "C" axis runs parallel to the length of the hexagonal crystal. Most gem corundum (sapphire and ruby) have a bipyramidal habit (shape) of the hexagonal crystal system. The habit will appear to be barrel-shaped if the two ends of the crystal are missing. When the hexagonal cross section is thick enough to cut a high-crowned cabochon, it should produce a good star if the needle structure is well formed. If the needle structure is not well formed or complete, you will have an imperfect star. It may still be chatoyant, but all six legs of the complete star will not be visible.

When you cannot identify the shape of the crystal because there are too few crystal faces, but the needle inclusions appear to be finely packed, you can rough-grind the stone into a sphere or partial sphere. A rough-ground stone will have a frosty finish. Dip the stone into a light oil so that you can check the needle structure. Examine the stone directly ***under*** a single shaft of light, either from a clear incandescent bulb or a single ray of sunlight. A frosted bulb or a fluorescent lamp will scatter the light. Turn the stone until lines start to form; the center of the star should be where any two lines across. Mark that spot with an aluminum marking stylus or with a spot of India ink. If no star lines appear, you will have to grind the stone into a complete sphere.

Once you orient the star, cut the base of the cabochon parallel to the spot marked on the stone. After you establish the base of the stone, finish the cabochon, following the usual procedures of grinding, sanding, and polishing. If the gemstone is 8 or more in hardness, use diamond abrasives. Because silicon carbide wheels and corundum (ruby and sapphire) are approximately the same hardness, the wheels will wear rapidly and grinding the gemstone will be slow and tedious. If you cannot use diamond abrasives with your cabochon unit, you can buy a set of four to six small hard wood wheels that can handle all grades of diamond abrasives.

Four-rayed star stones can be oriented by the same process as the six-rayed stones. The gemstones producing most of the four-rayed stars belong to the cubic crystal system, such as garnet. Because of its complex crystal habits, garnet has been known to produce even an eight- or twelve-rayed star, but this is rare.

In addition to the corundums (ruby and sapphire), rose quartz, beryl (aquamarine), and diopside occasionally produce star stones. Cat's-eyes may occur in moonstone (feldspar), but stars in moonstone are rare.

Cat's-eye Stones

The needle structure of a cat's-eye is oriented in one direction. The silk, or needles, are oriented parallel to the "C" axis, which is the length of the crystal. Orienting cat's-eye stones is not as difficult as orienting star stones. Some transparent gemstones occasionally will appear to be chatoyant or to have a strong sheen, but, unless the tubular or needle structure is tightly packed, you will not be able to obtain a sharp cat's-eye and the stone will show only a broad, hazy chatoyance. Chrysoberyl cat's-eyes are the best known stones and, when the eye is sharp, they are the most expensive.

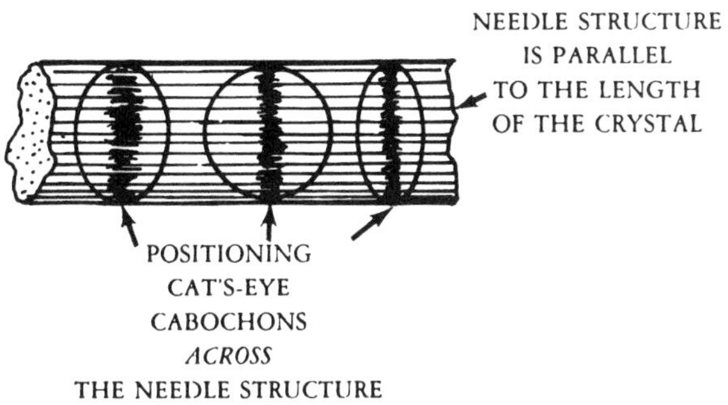

Fig. 4-13 Positioning and orienting a cat's-eye cabochon. For a good cat's-eye, the needle structure should be tightly packed. Illustration by Dara E. Yost.

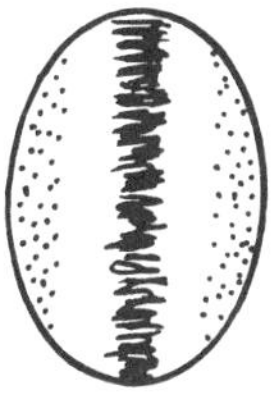

Fig. 4-14 The ends of needle structures are visible on the sides of a cabochon. The dots represent the ends of the fibers. Illustration by Dara E. Yost.

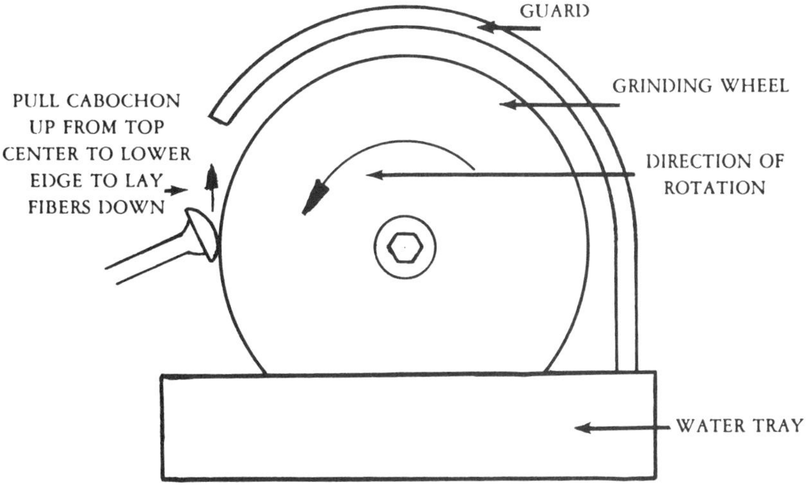

Fig. 4-15 To smooth down the fibers, the center of the cabochon should be placed against the wheel and the stone pulled up to follow the curve of the cabochon. This is an end view of the grinding wheel. Illustration by Dara E. Yost.

Besides chrysoberyl, other stones that sometimes produce cat's-eyes are tourmaline, some varieties of beryl (aquamarine, light green beryl and, rarely, morganite, a pink variety), williamsite (serpentine), apatite, sillimanite (fibrolite), iolite, sapphire (corundum), enstatite, and tigereye.

A cat's-eye stone can be cut as an oval or round cabochon. The stone should be oriented so that the cat's-eye is well centered when looking *straight down* on the top of the stone under an incandescent light or under a ray or sunlight. As the stone is tipped from side to side or from end to end, the light will reflect a cat's-eye.

In many cat's-eye stones, the needles or tubes are hollow. You must take preventive measures before making the first saw cuts to section the stone to ensure that the ends of the tubular structures do not fill with grit or polish, since the ends are visible on either side of the finished stone. If possible, use only clear water to lubricate the saw. Otherwise, soak the stone in water overnight. Adding a small amount of detergent will increase capillary action, permitting the water to fill the tubular structures.

Another way to seal the coarse tubular structures is to fill the pores with water-glass, a sodium-silicate solution. Warm the water-glass solution and add a small amount of detergent. Immerse the stone and leave it overnight. The next day, remove the stone and allow it to dry out. Repeat this process until the tubular structures appear to be filled.

When grinding and polishing, start from the center of the top of the gemstone, placing it against the wheels and pulling the stone up. Work from the top of the stone to the base, so that the fiber ends become smoothed down. Starting from the edge of the base of the stone will pull into the fibers, opening them up instead of smoothing them down.

Once you have ground it to shape and sanded it, examine the stone carefully. If the fibers have opened up, thoroughly clean and resoak the stone in the water-glass solution to fill the tubular structures before polishing the stone. Select a polish that will blend with the body color of the stone. If the stone is colorless, use a white polish. If the stone has a pinkish cast, try cerium oxide. For medium to dark green stones, use chrome oxide. Most experienced hobbyists have a selection of polishes and a leather disc for each polish. Remember, never mix polishes on the same polishing disc.

Play of Color (Opal)

The play of color in precious opal is caused by the series of closely packed spheres of different sizes. Because the sizes of the spheres vary, voids are cre-

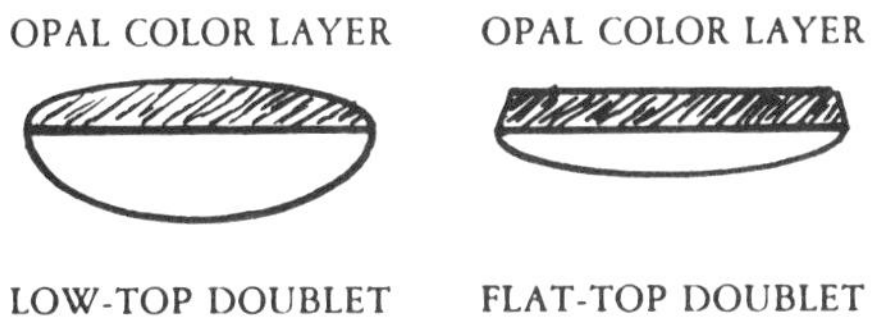

Fig. 4-16 A side view of two types of opal doublets that are made when the play-of-color layer is very thin. Illustration by Dara E. Yost.

ated. Light rays striking the voids are diffracted, resulting in the play of color. The play of color in some pieces of opal covers the full spectrum of colors, from red through violet. Some colors may be more predominant than others. The color in opal, especially in Australian opal, is often formed in layers or seams. The seams of color vary in thickness, and some opal will have color throughout the entire piece. When opal is layered, you must orient the stone so that the color layer and the base of the cabochon are parallel.

Establish the base of the cabochon and mark it with a stylus or a spot of India ink; then check to see that the saw cut will parallel the color layer. If the color layer is thin in spots, leave some of the plain opal under the color layer to add strength to the cabochon. Some hobbyists remove the plain opal, or "potch," from the top of the color layer first so that they can more easily determine the thickness of the bottom or base of the cabochon. If the top layer of potch is fairly thick, making a thin cut on the trim saw may remove most of it, or grind off the potch so that you can see the direction of the color layer. After you have exposed most of the color, decide what size or shape to make the cabochon, or whether to cut a free-form cabochon to retain as much of the color as possible.

Opal is 5 in hardness and is heat-sensitive. Use caution when dopping the stone. Friction heat builds rapidly, so use plenty of water on the grinding wheels and sanding drums and watch the stone carefully. If too much heat builds up during dopping, grinding, or polishing, very fine crack marks (called crazing) may develop. Opal will polish well on a hard felt wheel with either tin oxide or cerium oxide.

If you do not have a hard felt wheel, use a leather disc on an end faceplate. Hold the stone against the wheels, sanding drums, and polishing wheel or disc with a light pressure. Be careful when you remove the finished stone from the dop stick.

When the color layer is thin and you leave a backing of potch to reinforce the opal, or when you have added other material to the bottom of the stone for support, the top of the opal is often polished flat instead of with the usual low or high dome.

Labradorescence

Labradorite, a variety of feldspar, is 6 in hardness and has a distinct cleavage. As a result, it is slightly heat-sensitive. With caution, you can use standard dopping procedures.

To locate the labradorescence (a broad flash of iridescent deep blue or blue-violet, or greenish blue or greenish yellow), use either a clear incandescent light bulb or sunlight positioned directly above. Looking *straight down* on the stone, turn it in all directions until you find the flash of color. Mark the surface where the color flash occurs. The base of the cabochon should be cut or ground parallel to the flash of color.

If the rough material is thick, you may be able to cut some of it off with a trim saw. Even when you trim as close as possible, there may still be a triangular area that cannot be trimmed with a saw. Grind this material with the grinding wheel until the base of the cabochon is parallel to the flash of color.

Once you have established the base of the cabochon, continue with the usual methods of cutting a cabochon. Remember, labradorite is slightly heat-sensitive, so be careful when cutting and polishing.

Gemstones that show the optical phenomena of aventurescence and iridescence can usually be treated in the same way as labradorite.

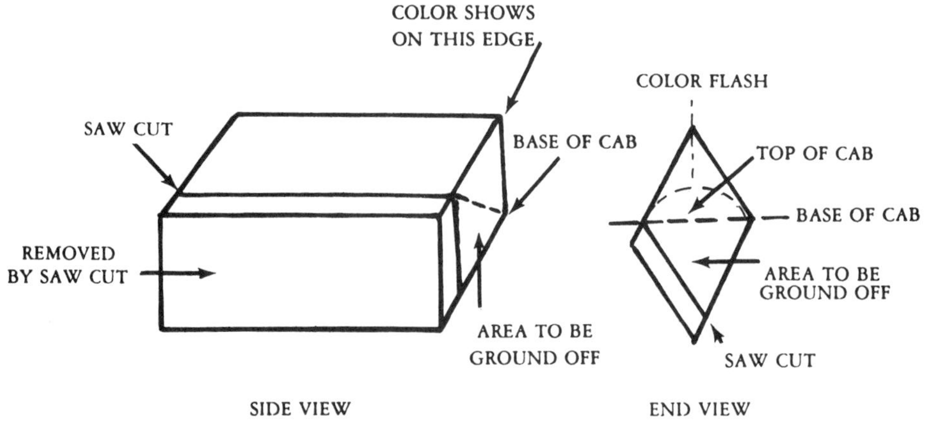

Fig. 4-17 Orienting labordorescence: at left is a piece of labradorite rough, showing where the saw cut should be made. At right is the end view, showing the placement of the cabochon and the part that probably will have to be ground off. Illustration by Dara E. Yost.

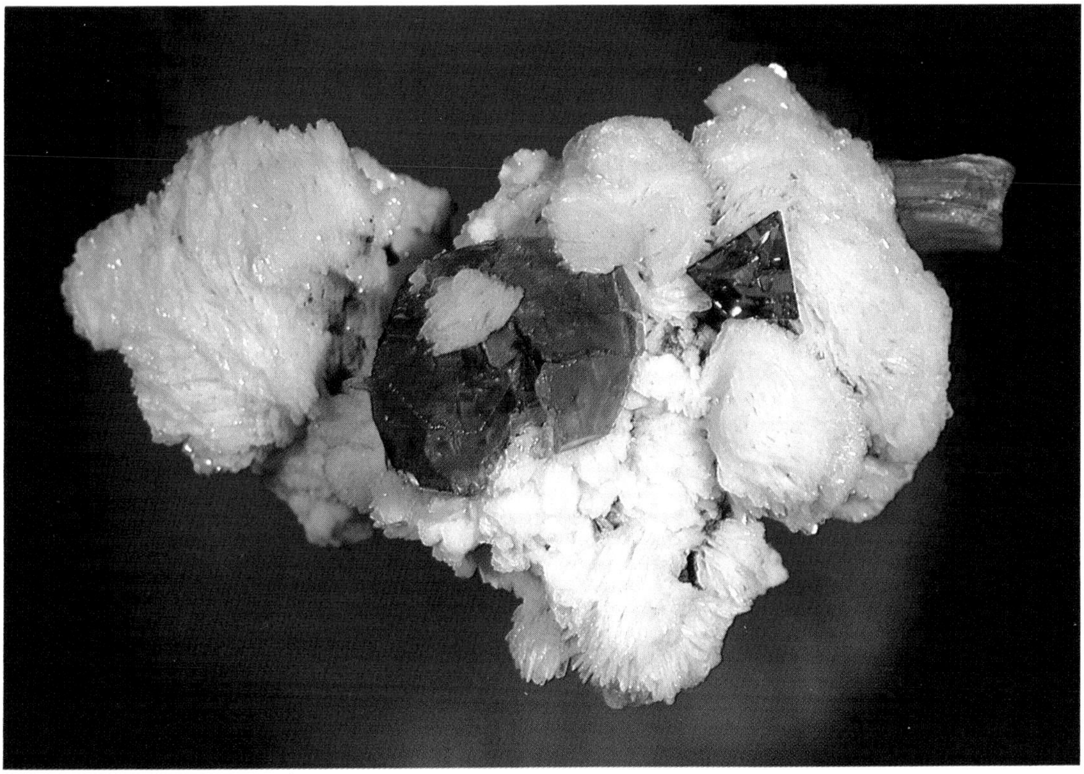

Fig. 1 Cut stone and mineral specimen of spessartite garnet from Ramona, California. Photograph by Laura J. Ramsey.

Fig. 2 A rough imperial topaz and a cut stone from Oro Preto, Brazil. Photograph by Laura J. Ramsey.

Fig. 3 Four Brazilian tourmalines. Left to right: indicolite, blue-green tourmaline, pink tourmaline, and rubellite. Photograph by Laura J. Ramsey.

Fig. 4 A fine kunzite of superior quality, slightly over 500 carats, with the dopped preform and a rough specimen, cut by John Ramsey. Photograph by Laura J. Ramsey.

Fig. 5 Faceted amethyst-citrine (bicolor quartz), also called "ametrine" or "trystine," and a rough specimen. Photograph by Laura J. Ramsey.

Fig. 6 A fine-quality aquamarine. Photograph by Laura J. Ramsey.

Fig. 7 A chrysoberyl slightly over 47 carats, cut by John Ramsey. Photograph by Laura J. Ramsey.

Fig. 8 One of the largest faceted magnesites, weighing slightly over 100 carats, cut by John Ramsey. Photograph by Laura J. Ramsey.

Fig. 9 A morganite (beryl) with an exceptional color, weighing slightly over 200 carats. Photograph by Laura J. Ramsey.

Fig. 10 A large aquamarine from Brazil weighing over 150 carats. Photograph by Laura J. Ramsey.

Fig. 11 A free-form yellow fluorite, cut by John Ramsey. Photograph by Laura J. Ramsey.

Fig. 12 Tumbled stones can be used to form floral pictures. The stones in these two pictures are amethyst, carnelian, and white and green agate. Collection of the author. Courtesy, The Rock Farm. Photograph by A. D. Daegling, Jr.

Fig. 13 Three unusual cabochons of Brazilian agate, designed, cut, and polished by Bernard N. Kronberg. Left to right: the Cross of Peace, from Pope John Paul's robe; the traditional fleur-de-lis; and a Cross Crosslet from the Crown of Denmark. Photograph by the artist.

Fig. 14 Four stylized leaf patterns inspired by oak and maple autumn leaves, designed, cut, and polished by Bernard N. Kronberg. Photograph by the artist.

Fig. 15 A carved figurine of Brazilian quartz with rhodochrosite trim on the headdress and front of the dress and the base, carved by Opal Maline. Photograph by Maury Maline.

Fig. 16 Spirit of St. Louis, faceted in Brazilian rock crystal, by Jerry Muchna. Its total weight is 880 carats; it has 695 facets, which required 179 hours to complete. Photograph by Bob Jones.

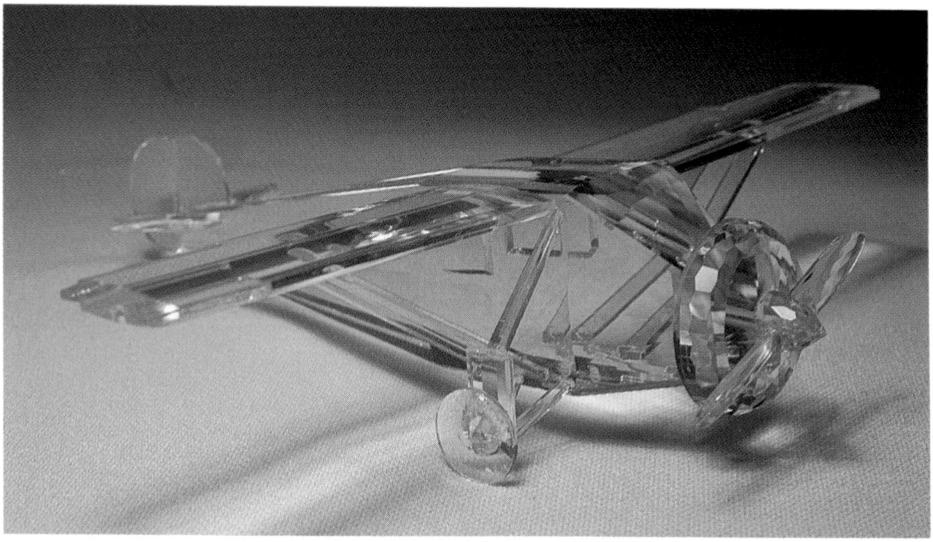

Soft Organic Gemstones: Amber, Coral, and Ivory

AMBER

Amber, a fossil resin used for cabochons, beads, and carving, is only 2 in hardness, so it is extremely heat-sensitive and chips easily. It can be worked by hand and will cut easily with a hacksaw, or it can be shaped with a No. 2 steel file, wet-sanded with a 320 "Wet or Dry" sanding cloth, and finished on a 400 or 600 grit wet sanding cloth. Polish amber on a leather buff or a felt wheel or pad with tin oxide or cerium oxide.

If you use lapidary equipment, use a light pressure and run the machines as slowly as possible. If the polishing wheel causes too much friction heat, turn off the motor and polish by hand. Use plenty of water when grinding and sanding. When amber begins to get warm, it may become sticky and clog the wheels and sanding cloth. When working amber by hand with files, you will have to stop and clean the files frequently with a wire brush.

CORAL

Gem coral is calcium carbonate, an organic material, and is 3½ in hardness. It can range in color from white to dark red. Gem coral can be cut and polished on a regular cabochon unit, but you must be careful when dopping since it is heat-sensitive. Be careful not to grind too deeply or too much at a time or you will wear away too much of the stone. Use only a fine-grinding wheel that has been dressed down to a smooth even surface, and keep plenty of water on the grinding wheels and sanding cloth. Hold the stone against the wheels and sanding cloth with a light pressure. Coral requires a 400 or 600 grit wet sanding cloth for the final sanding. It can be polished on either a hard felt wheel or a leather disc with tin oxide or cerium oxide.

Black and gold corals are a horny substance and when cut cross-grain show a ring structure similar to the growth rings of a tree. They are even more heat-sensitive than the white, pink, and red corals. With caution, black and gold coral can be dopped, using regular methods. The coral can be shaped on a smooth 320 grinding wheel, using the slowest speed. Sand with a 400 or 600 grit wet sanding cloth and use plenty of water.

Black and gold coral can be wet-sanded just as easily by hand. Watch carefully as you work to prevent any friction heat from developing. If too much friction heat builds up, reddish brown splotches will appear on the surfaces. Removing the splotches involves regrinding, resanding, and repolishing.

Black and gold coral should be prepolished using tripoli or white diamond on a clean soft cotton flannel buff before going to the polishing stage. The cotton flannel buff will build heat rapidly; be careful! Polish black coral with black jewelers rouge, which can be purchased in stick form. Apply it sparingly because it tends to load the cotton flannel buff quickly. If you want to accentuate the growth rings, use one of the white polishing powders, either tin oxide or Linde A. Some of the white in the growth rings will create an attractive pattern against the black color.

Gold coral can be handled the same as the black coral, using only a white polish. Gold coral is rare and at present is only used commercially.

IVORY

Note: Ivory is subject to strict federal regulations regarding importation and may not be available to the lapidary hobbyist (see the Appendix).

Ivory is only 2½ in hardness and must be handled with moderate caution when dopping, grinding, sanding, and polishing. Use only a smooth fine-grinding wheel, 400 and 600 grit dry sanding cloth, and very little pressure. Use plenty of water in all of the grinding and sanding processes. Friction heat can cause ivory to discolor. Ivory will polish easily with tin oxide on a hard felt wheel or a leather faceplate, or it can be worked easily by hand or cut with a hacksaw and shaped with steel files. Do not use a hand file any coarser than a No. 2 (2/0 cut).

For the sanding, use 400 and 600 grit sanding cloth with plenty of water. Before going to the polish, prepolish with a piece of crocus cloth dry. Crocus cloth is used by jewelry makers on metals in the prepolish stage. Ivory can be polished with tin oxide on a hard felt wheel or leather disc. When working ivory by hand, use a hand-held soft leather disc. Ivory can be carved or used for scrimshaw and inlay work.

5

EQUIPMENT FOR CABOCHON CUTTING

In the early days hobbyists had to build their own equipment for cutting and polishing cabochons. Today the situation is different. Hobbyists can purchase several types of saws and blades, as well as special electric cabochon-making units. You can even buy a complete saw kit and make it yourself.

DIAMOND SLAB SAWS

Slab saws of different sizes are used in lapidary work to cut chunks or blocks of rock into slabs or other forms, such as squares or bookends, and for cutting geodes and nodules in half or into slices. The smaller saws are used for cutting the slabs into other shapes. All slab saws, regardless of size, are designed for diamond blades.

Mud saws were the forerunners of the diamond saws but were slow and tiresome to operate. The early mud saw was simply a hand-held frame with a wire (sometimes a fine twisted wire) stretched across the opening of the "C" shaped frame, with handles on both ends. Since the wire was flexible, it usually required one person on each end of the saw frame to draw the wire back and forth across the rock. A third person had to stand by the boulder and feed water and abrasive (quartz, garnet, or corundum) under the wire.

Mud saws have been modernized and improved and today use either silicon carbide or diamond abrasives. They are still used today when boulders are too large to transport from the field. A portable saw with a large-diameter diamond blade can be set up in the field and powered by a gasoline engine, an electrical motor, or water power.

During the summer of 1969, William Munz was operating his jade claim in Kobuk, Alaska. He had extracted jade boulders that were too big to be put on the barges and transported downstream. He had to bring in by barge all the supplies and parts necessary to build the large saws at the claim camp. The saws were constructed so that the blades cut into the jade boulders from the side (Fig. 5-1). The boulders were then cut and sectioned into pieces small enough to fit on the barge.

Bill was able to operate two saws simultaneously. The saws were powered by water diverted from the river through flumes. When the saws were started

Fig. 5-1 These two 36-inch (91.44 cm) saws, constructed at the campsite of Bill Munz's Alaskan jade claim, were designed to run in tandem, powered by a Pelton waterpower unit. Water was brought to the camp by water flumes from the river. Courtesy, William Munz and the Lapidary Journal, Inc.

Fig. 5-2 An electric 36-inch (91.44 cm) saw, powered by an auxiliary generator, which was also constructed on the site. Courtesy, William Munz and the Lapidary Journal, Inc.

correctly, Bill was able to run them in tandem all night without keeping the camp awake.

A separate 36-inch (91.44 cm) electric saw was also constructed on the site (Fig. 5-2). The electricity was supplied by a small generator which also was built on the camp site. The saw was built with a movable carriage and an overhead frame so that the saw blade could cut across the top of the boulder. The jade was then hoisted on the movable carriage.

The next winter, while Bill was back at his winter quarters in the southern part of the United States, he built a 96-inch (243.84 cm) saw blade and equipped it with a special MK diamond-segmented blade rim 12 inches (30.48

cm) wide and 0.125 inches (3.175 mm) thick, with the diamond segments spaced ¼ inch (6.35 mm) between segments. This large saw ran well with a minimum of difficulties. One of the first large boulders he cut with this saw weighed 7,000 pounds. Clear water was the only lubricant used with any of the large saws.

Although 36-inch (91.44 cm) saws are available, the hobbyist's workshop rarely requires anything larger than an 18-inch (45.72 cm) diamond saw, unless the hobbyist wishes to specialize in making large spheres or bookends. Saws are sold by the size of the diamond blade.

Fig. 5-3 An 18-inch (45.72 cm) saw with an extra assembly attached to the saw vise to hold geode halves firmly while the slabs are cut off. Courtesy, Fran-Tom Lapidary Equipment, Division of Contempo Enterprises.

A diamond saw consists of a steel frame and a steel saw box that holds the lubricant for the blade. An 18-inch (45.72 cm) saw usually requires a box 11¼ inches (28.575 cm) deep, at least 25¾ inches (65.405 cm) wide, and 34 inches (86.36 cm) long. Several inches below the top of the box is the saw blade arbor, made of cold-rolled steel machined to 1 inch (2.54 cm) in diameter. Steel flanges hold the blade firmly in position. Arbor bearings are usually lubricated and sealed at the factory to protect against grit and sludge when sawing the rock. The vise that holds the rock has cast-iron jaws lined with hardwood faceplates for better gripping of the rock and for ease in replacement. The carriage rides on sturdy, well-constructed rods.

Some 18-inch (45.72 cm) saws have a three-speed powerfeed carriage run by a ¾ horsepower motor with reset overload protection (Fig. 5-3). The powerfeed mechanism is connected to the motor pulley by V-belts, and the motor-mount platform is located below the saw on a platform close to the V-belts. All belts and pulleys are enclosed for safety. These large saws can be purchased with a plastic or metal hood or with a plastic window in a metal hood. Slab saws can be purchased with or without the blade and motor.

The rectangular box serves as a tank for the saw-blade lubricant. The spinning action keeps the blade and rock lubricated. Several lubricants are available. One of the first lubricants was kerosene and water, but rust was always a problem. A thin flushing oil lubricates well and prevents rust. Use a flushing oil that contains no PCBs (polychlorinated biphenyls). Transformer oils are more likely to contain PCBs than flushing oils. All lubricants create an odor as the saw cuts. Breathing the mist or fumes from an oil that contains PCBs is hazardous, so make sure that your workshop is always well ventilated. If you are sensitive to the fumes, wear a breathing mask.

An 18-inch (45.72 cm) saw is an excellent size for a club workshop, a school, or for the hobbyist who specializes in cutting geodes and making bookends. The next smaller size saw will handle as many as three sizes of saw blades: 16 inch (40.64 cm), 14 inch (35.56 cm), and 12 inch (30.48 cm).

TRIM SAWS

Trim saws, smaller than slab saws, are designed to sit on a workbench in the workshop or on a sturdy table. The blades range in size from 10 inches (25.4 cm) to 6 inches (15.24 cm) (Fig. 5-4). These smaller saws usually do not have a hood, but you can purchase one as an accessory. A blade-coolant deflector

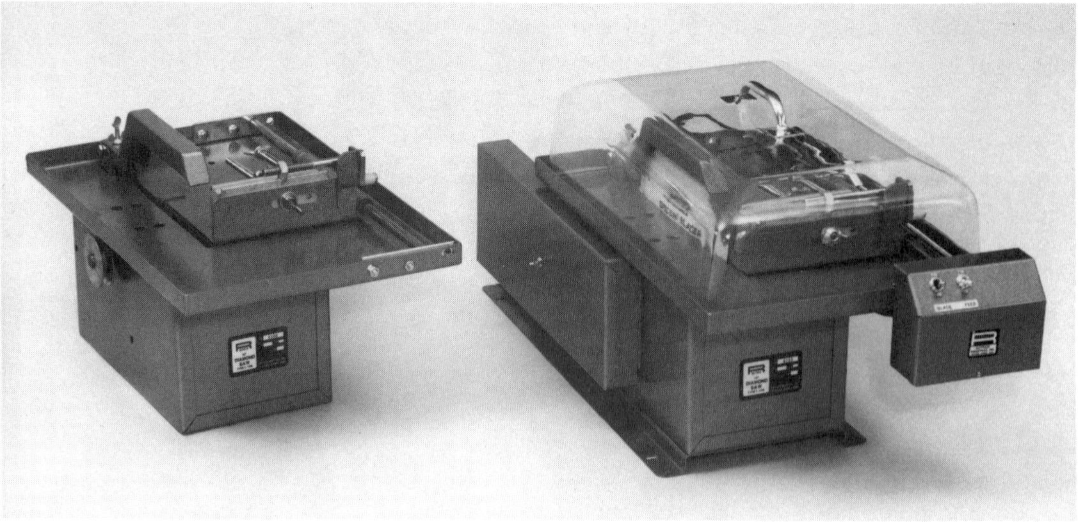

Fig. 5-4 Ten-inch (25.40 cm) trim saws are popular in the home workshops because they can be used to slice small rough pieces of rock, as well as used for trimming. The saw on the left has no belt guards or hood. Courtesy, Raytech Industries, Inc.

Fig. 5-5 A combination 8- and 10-inch (20.32 and 25.40 cm) saw is a versatile tool for a home workshop. Use the smaller blade to trim out a cabochon from a slab and the larger blade to slice pieces of rough stone. Courtesy, Covington Engineering Corp.

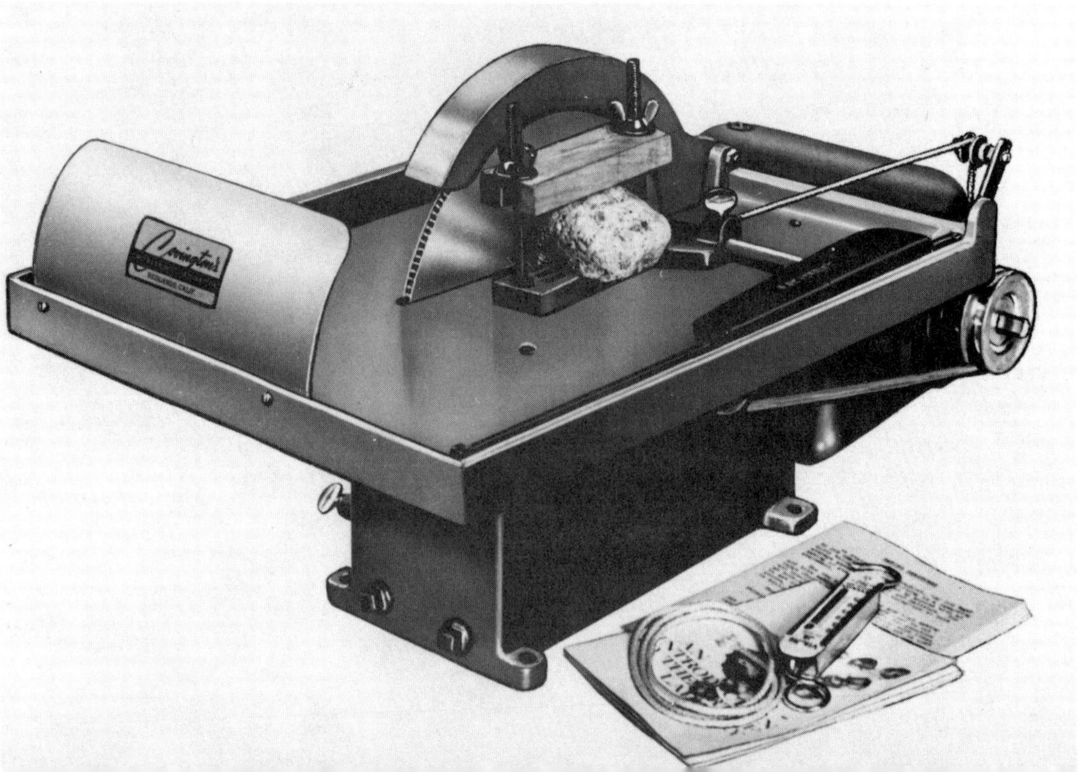

controls the lubricant, and a plastic shield is mounted across the front of the saw table. A rectangular tank holds the lubricant. Trim saws are usually made of cast aluminum with a vise made of steel plate and replaceable hardwood jaw facings. The vise, powered by a gravity feed, also has a cross-feed and runs on a guide mounted on the saw table. When shaping and trimming a cabochon or when faceting, you can rotate the vise off to the side. Some trim saws include a cabochon unit and are called an "all-in-one" unit or a "combination" unit (Fig. 5-5).

FACETER'S TRIM SAWS

A faceter's trim saw is the smallest size saw and is designed for a very thin blade made of either copper or steel, and will handle a 4-inch (10.16 cm) or 6-inch (15.24 cm) blade. It comes without a vise since most faceters hand-hold their gem rough, but you can purchase a vise as an accessory. The arbor shaft is ¼ inch (12.7 mm) cold-rolled steel. The bearings are lubricated and sealed by the manufacturer. The blade-arbor hole size can also be ½ inch (12.7 mm) or ⅝ inch (15.87mm).

SAW KITS

Saw kits are available for both slab saws and trim saws. Kits include the arbor, bearings, and vise assembly—everything except the saw housing and stand (Fig. 5-6). Plans and complete instructions for building a wood-frame housing and a sealed tank for holding the oil lubricant come with the kit. If you like to build your own equipment, a saw kit is the answer.

SETTING UP A SLAB OR TRIM SAW

A new slab or trim saw rarely needs to be adjusted if you set it up on a solid, level surface and follow the manufacturer's instructions. Under those conditions, the saw will give many years of good service before the arbor assembly will need any repairs.

If you purchase a floor model, the floor of your workshop must be solid and level. If your workshop has a wooden floor, you may have to build a spe-

Fig. 5-6 A 20-inch (50.8 cm) saw kit for the do-it-yourself hobbyist. Courtesy, Mohave Industries, Inc.

cial heavy platform. You must place the saw on a solid surface so that no vibration will occur, which will cause unnecessary wear on the blades as well as on the saw arbor and shaft. The carriage-vise assembly ***must*** travel parallel to the arbor on which the diamond blade is mounted. Trim and slab saws, regardless of size, are designed to make straight cuts only. *Do not* try to cut curves or you will damage the blade.

BUYING A USED SAW

When buying a used saw, check the arbor shaft before putting on a new blade. Take hold of the arbor shaft at the blade end and try to move it back and forth. Any movement of the arbor shaft indicates radial play. An arbor shaft in good condition should spin freely. Also check for axial play by trying to move the shaft in and out. Any movement here indicates axial play. If either radial or axial play exists, the saw blade will not cut properly. You will have to have the arbor shaft repaired before installing a new blade.

Before putting a new blade in the saw, check both blade flanges for any burns or gouges on the surface of the flanges that hold the diamond blade. If burns or gouges exist, the flanges can be resurfaced at a machine shop. When the flanges are placed together, no light should show through. If you can see light, the flange faces are not parallel and will have to be replaced or they will distort the blade.

Flanges or blade collars should measure at least ¼ (6.35 mm) of the diameter of the blade. They should contact the blade away from the center in order to hold it without distortion. When putting in the blade, tighten the arbor nut firmly but not so tightly that the flanges might collapse. Never grip the blade when tightening the nut; instead, grasp the arbor to get the leverage you need.

Be sure to check the belts. On a trim saw the belt should squeeze in approximately ½ inch (12.7 mm); on a slab saw the belt should squeeze in about 1 inch (25.40 mm).

Check the electrical cord for any breaks, frayed insulation, or bare wires before plugging it in. The cord should be as short as possible and still reach from the saw to the wall plug without any coiled cord laying on the floor. If the motor has been installed by someone other than the manufacturer, check to see if the horsepower is the same as that listed in the saw specifications.

SAW BLADES

Diamond saw blades are manufactured in a variety of sizes and types for different uses. A notched, rimmed blade is popular with lapidaries because it is so durable. Blades are made from four basic materials: diamond, powdered metal, silver solder, and high-grade steel core. In the past, manufacturers used crushed industrial-grade natural diamond. Most manufacturers today use man-made diamond because of its superior cutting qualities. Steel cores are used because of their excellent tensioning characteristics. Silver solder is used as a binder because of its greater fusibility. The powdered metal distributes the diamond uniformly in the rim notches of the blade, which are impregnated with the silver solder.

Selecting the correct blade for the material you are cutting is essential. If you will use the saw to slab dense material such as Brazilian agate, petrified wood, jaspers, and most agates, or when the loss of material is not critical, use a standard rim blade with a heavier blade core. If loss of material is a factor, as it is in faceting, select a premium notched rim or a continuous rim blade and perhaps a thinner-cored blade. If you are faceting and using a faceter's trim saw, you may want to order a 4- or 6-inch (10.6 or 15.24 cm) blade with a very thin core.

If you are setting up a slab saw in a classroom workshop where a number of hobbyists will be operating the saw, use the standard blade with a heavier steel core. Saw blade speeds are expressed by either revolutions per minute (RPM) or by surface feet per minute (SFPM). When you purchase saw blades, check with your dealer about the proper speed.

SAW-BLADE LUBRICANTS

Diamond blades cannot be operated without a lubricant. In addition to a thin flushing oil, some hobbyists prefer a water-soluble oil. Pour the lubricant into the tank until the blade is immersed about ⅜ inch (9.525 mm). This will allow the spinning blade to pick up the correct amount of lubricant to keep the saw cut clean of sludge.

Check the lubricant frequently. When it begins to get too dirty or full of sludge, the blade will not operate efficiently. Pour out or drain the old lubricant, clean all the sludge from the saw tank, and add fresh lubricant. Some hobbyists pour or drain the old oil into a plastic or metal container and allow the sludge to settle to the bottom. When the oil in the container has separated from the sludge (it may take a day or two), you can siphon the clear oil from the top and reuse it, adding fresh oil to bring the oil level to the proper height on the saw blade. Dispose of the sludge in a plastic container.

A good time to check the blade for flutter is when the lubricant tank is empty. Normal blade flutter should never be more than 0.0005 inch (0.0127 mm) per inch of blade diameter. If the blade has more flutter, either the blade or the saw may need to be repaired.

BREAKING IN THE SAW BLADE

A new diamond blade must be broken in before regular use. Make several cuts through a soft abrasive material, such as a common red brick. The soft abrasive will bring the rim of the blade into concentricity with the arbor and will "open up" the blade rim by increasing the diamond protrusion.

To start a saw cut on the rock, run the saw blade at operating speed and feed the rock into the spinning blade very slowly. Watch the initial cut to make certain the rock is being fed in straight. If it is not, the blade will deflect at the point of contact. If the blade deflects, you will have an uneven cut, and the blade will be "dished" by the time you finish the cut. If the blade begins to deflect, stop the saw and shift the rock a little to one side or the other and start again. If the blade becomes "dished," it will have to be repaired.

USING THE SAW

When sawing dense material such as agate or petrified wood, the rock may break just as you are about to finish the cut, leaving a jagged small nub. To prevent this, stop the saw near the end of the cut. If you do not stop the saw in time and the nub or spur goes past the saw blade, it can permanently damage and weaken the core of the blade (see Fig. 5-7).

Slab saws usually have a cut-off mechanism that can be set to stop the saw just before you finish the cut or before a break occurs. If you are using a trim saw, release the pressure close to the end of the cut. Most trim saws that have a vise assembly have a gravity feed. When using a gravity feed, watch it closely and when it nears the end of the cut, turn the saw off. Remove the vise assembly and feed the stone into the saw by hand to finish the cut. This will allow you to stop the cut quickly if the stone begins to crack.

Dense materials such as agate or jasper will take much longer to cut than obsidian or a similar, less dense material. Never force a saw blade to cut at a speed faster than its normal operating speed. Occasionally a diamond blade

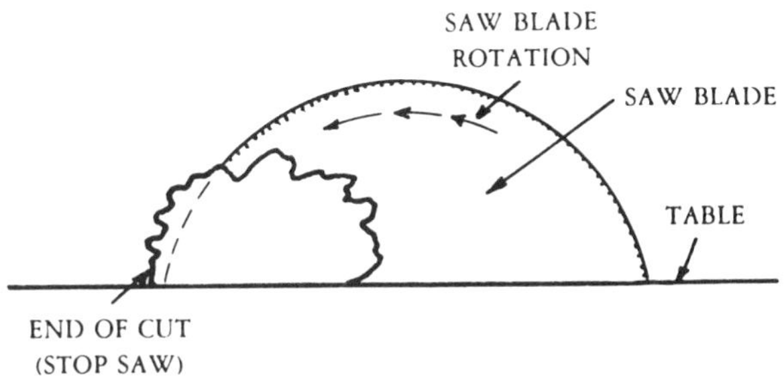

Fig. 5-7 Toward the end of a saw cut, the gem material may break and the nubbin of rock could damage the saw blade. Always stop the saw just before finishing the cut. Illustration by Dara E. Yost.

will glaze, just as a grinding wheel does. When this occurs, make several cuts through a red brick before sawing the rock. The soft abrasive quality of the brick will abrade some of the metal bond on the rim of the blade and increase the diamond protrusion.

Reverse the saw blade periodically to ensure even wear. Forcing rock through a saw can cause wear on the arbor and shaft, as well as on the blade, and could stall the motor.

Never leave the saw running without constant supervision; too many unexpected situations can occur. If the saw blade hits an invisible fracture in the rock, the rock may shift slightly, and the shift could be enough to dish the blade or stall the saw. If the hum of the saw changes, stop the saw immediately, back the saw vise away from the blade, reposition the rock in the vise, and start the saw again.

CABOCHON-GRINDING UNITS

The hobbyist has a wide range of cabochon equipment to choose from. Combination units and individual arbors come in several sizes and variations (see Figs. 5-8 and 5-9).

Some combination units require a relatively small amount of space in a home workshop. Two different units are available. One uses silicon carbide

Fig. 5-8 A small compact unit for cutting and polishing a cabochon. The 6-inch (15.24 cm) coarse wheel can be replaced with a fine grinding wheel, a faceplate for sanding, and a leather-covered faceplate for polishing. Courtesy, MDR Manufacturing Co.

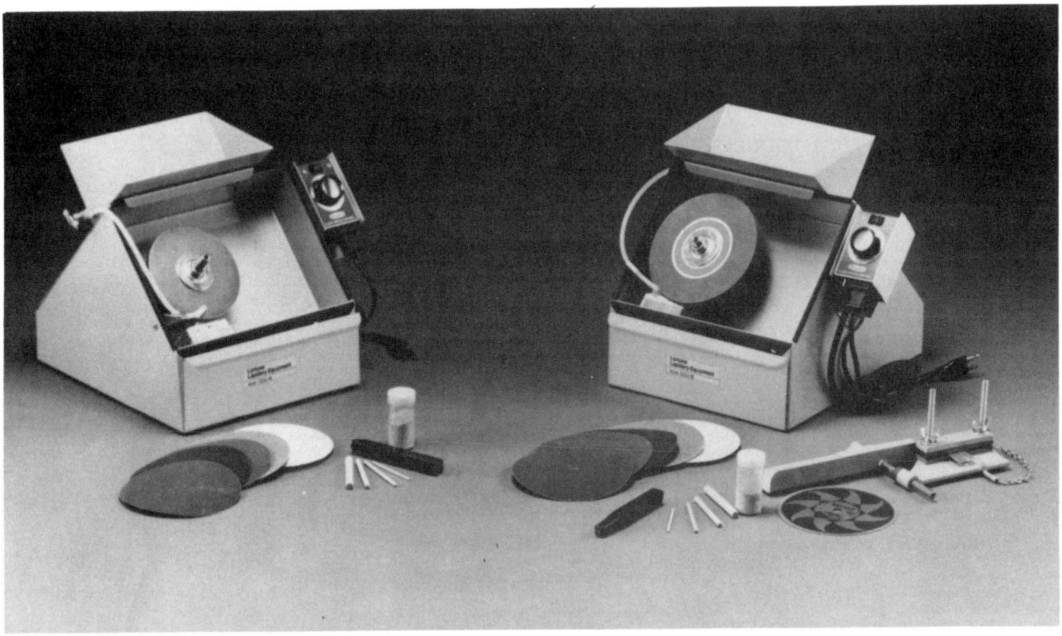

Fig. 5-9 All phases of cutting and polishing can be accomplished by changing the wheel and discs on this compact unit. It can be used with either silicon carbide or diamond accessories. Courtesy, Lortone, Inc.

grinding wheels and sanding cloth. The other type is designed strictly for diamond wheels, diamond sanding, and diamond polishing. Diamond units are less noisy than the silicon carbide units, but they are also more expensive. With proper care, however, diamond wheels and polishing pads will last longer.

Before selecting equipment, consider the noise level and determine how much space you have. These are extremely important decisions if you live in a mobile home, condominium, or apartment. Try to attend a lapidary class to get a little experience before you buy your equipment. The best places to look for classes are the local gem and mineral clubs, adult education courses, or recreational centers that teach crafts. Most clubs or recreational facilities sponsoring lapidary workshops and classes have single arbors set up for each phase of grinding, sanding, and polishing so that several hobbyists can work at the same time. If classes are not available, try to attend a gem and mineral show where dealers display equipment.

Most silicon carbide complete units require less space than individual arbors. The unit is powered by a single motor. A unit with a saw blade larger than 6 to 8 inches (15.24 to 20.32 cm) might have a separate motor for the saw. Units come in two sizes: one for 8-inch (20.32 cm) wheels and one for 6-inch (15.24 cm) wheels. The 6-inch unit is more compact than the 8-inch unit. Combination units are available as stand models or complete bench models. If you have no running water in your workshop, you might want to install a recirculating pump and water reservoir to supply water to the grinding wheels and sanding drums.

SILICON CARBIDE WHEELS

Silicon carbide wheels require an even flow of water to keep them from clogging with grit from the rock. Before you start the grinding, turn on the motor, start the water, and let the wheels become thoroughly wet. When the grinding is finished, turn off the water and allow the wheels to spin dry (10 to 15 minutes). If you turn off the wheels and water at the same time, the water will collect in the bottom of the wheels, causing them to load. The next time you start the wheels, they will be out of balance. Out-of-balance wheels will whip and pound as they revolve and will cause extra wear on the arbors, or the wheels may break while you are grinding the stone.

When you grind a cabochon on a silicon carbide wheel, work back and forth over the entire surface of the wheels to prevent grooves from developing and to prevent having to dress or change the wheels too frequently. Diamond wheel dressers and silicon carbide dressing sticks can be purchased from a lapidary supply store, a rock shop, or through a supply catalog.

Since silicon carbide wheels are a soft to medium bond, they tend to develop low spots if your grinding is uneven. If a wheel starts to develop low spots or grooves, work only on the high spots until the wheel becomes even. You can use a dressing stick (Fig. 5-10) or a smooth piece of agate to true up the wheel, working down the high spots until the grinding surface is even. The agate will not remove as much of the wheel surface as a dressing stick will.

When dressing a wheel, use a tool rest so that you can apply the wheel dresser (Fig. 5-11), either diamond or silicon carbide, to the wheel evenly and slowly to prevent gouging. Occasionally a grinding wheel will glaze. When that occurs, the wheel will not cut properly and you will have to dress the wheel down just enough to break the glaze. Although silicon carbide wheels are a

Fig. 5-10 Use coarse and fine dressing sticks to dress diamond wheels and metal diamond discs. Courtesy, Crystalite Corporation.

Fig. 5-11 Use a diamond wheel dresser to dress silicon carbide grinding wheels. Always use a tool rest when truing up a wheel. Courtesy, Crystalite Corporation.

soft to medium bond, do not replace them with hard-bonded wheels or steel-tool grinding wheels. Hard-bonded wheels will not grind the rocks.

DIAMOND COMBINATION UNITS

When space and noise are problems, consider one of the diamond units (Fig. 5-12). They are less noisy, take less space, and are cleaner to operate than silicon carbide units. Some diamond units are compact enough to set on a table or desk in a corner of a room (Figs. 5-13 and 5-14). One young hobbyist converted her spare bedroom into a workroom. She used a dressing table with drawers on both sides to hold a 6-inch (15.24 cm) diamond cabochon unit. She placed an unfinished wooden desk, the same height as the dressing table, next to the dressing table for the faceting machine, with a lap storage unit alongside, and stored the faceting accessories in the desk drawers.

In the last ten years, there have been many changes and improvements in diamond cabochon combination units and diamond products. A good selection of cabochon units is now available at reasonable prices. Units with 4-inch (10.16 cm), 6-inch (15.24 cm), or 8-inch (20.32 cm) wheels come in several different combinations, and replacement wheels and accessories are easy to obtain. Most units have from one to six wheels of different grit or micron sizes. Cabochon-grinding wheels are designated by *grit size*. Cabochon-grinding wheels vary from 80 grit to 600 grit and as high as 3,000 in diamond abrasive, depending upon the number of wheels on the unit.

Fig. 5-12 This unit has (left to right) a 325-coarse grinding diamond crystalring, a 1,200 diamond crystalring for fine grinding, a resin bonded crystalsheen wheel for sanding, a finer crystalsheen wheel for a semipolish, and a polishing faceplate with 50,000 diamond. A stone can be completed without changing any wheels. Courtesy, Crystalite Corporation.

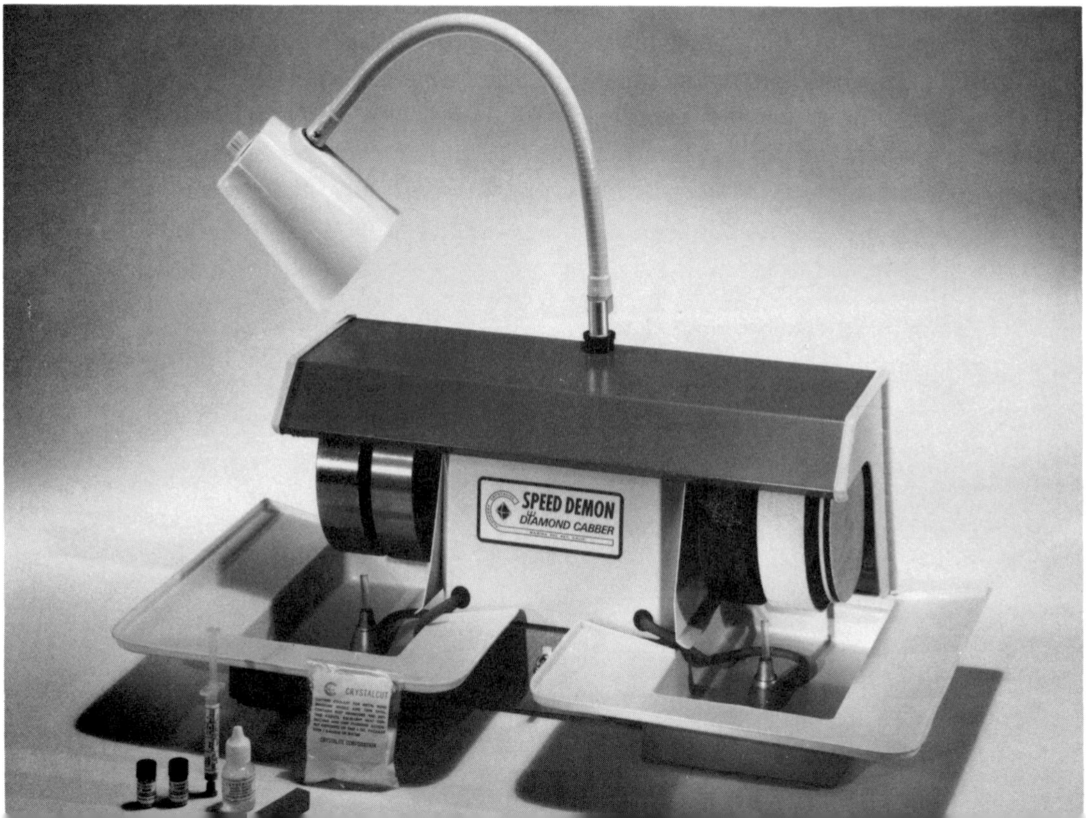

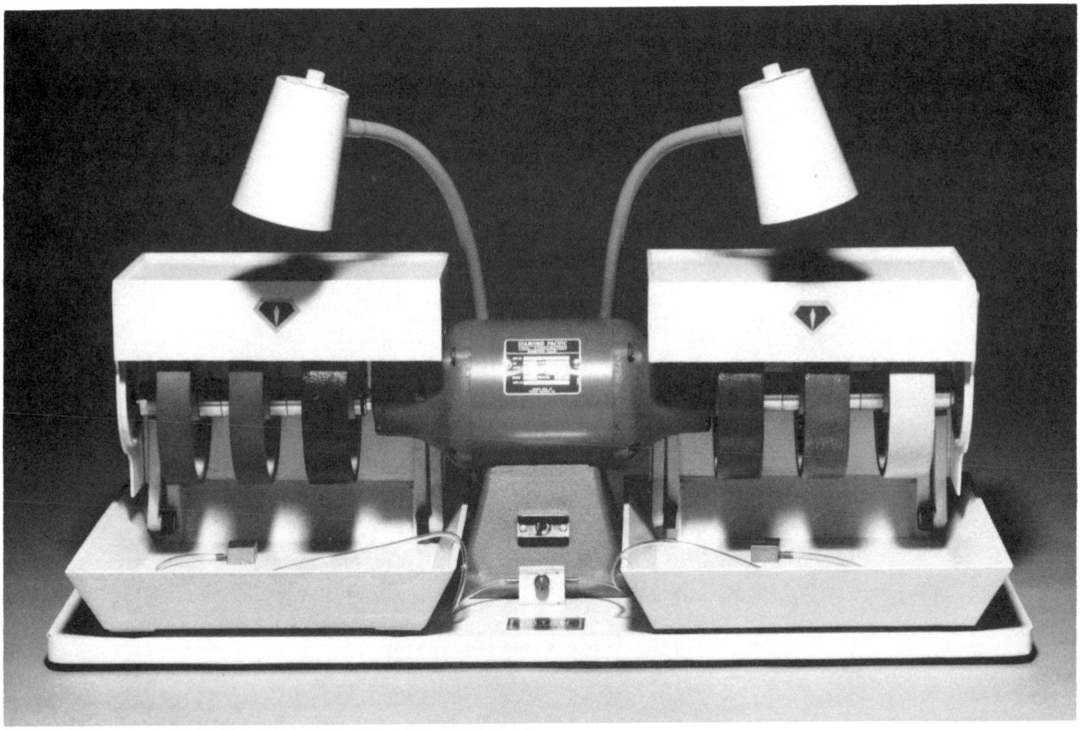

Fig. 5-13 This bench-model unit has diamond grinding wheels and polishing wheels to complete a stone. From left to right: wheels for the coarse grind, fine grind, and coarse sanding; the wheels for fine sanding, prepolishing, and final polishing. Courtesy, Diamond Pacific Tool Corporation.

WORKSHOP TIPS

One possibility for a home workshop would be to install a bench close to the laundry tub. This would provide access to running water for the silicon carbide grinding wheels. Install a 6- to 10-inch (15.24 to 25.4cm) trim saw on one end of the bench so that you have plenty of working space around the saw. Then set up separate arbors for sanding and polishing. The sanding arbor can be set up with two sanding drums, and the polishing arbor will hold your hard felt wheel and a sponge-rubber faceplate for your leather polishing discs. (The leather discs can be changed easily for different polishes, using a pressure-sensitive cement that holds the disc to the sponge-rubber backing of the faceplate. Most lapidary supply stores carry a variety of cements.) Mount a separate motor for each arbor underneath the workbench.

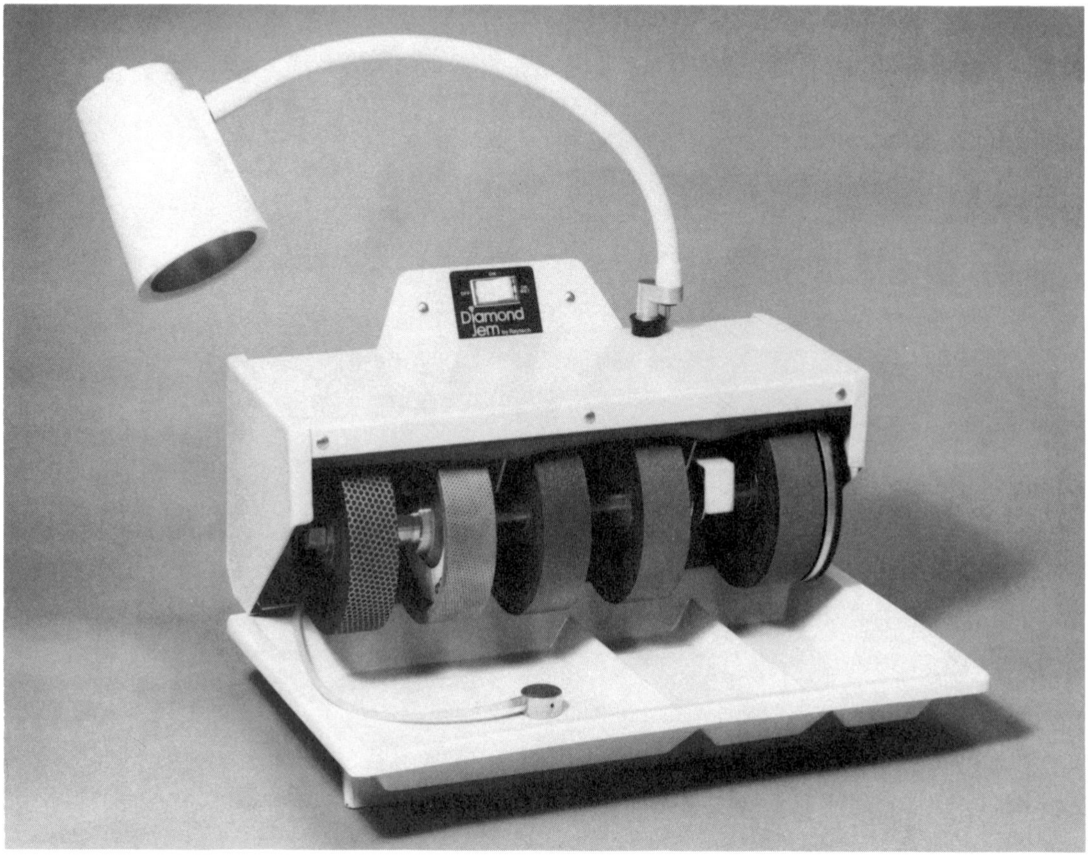

Fig. 5-14 This compact table-model diamond unit has wheels for grinding, sanding, and polishing. Courtesy, Raytech Industries, Inc.

If you are considering a diamond unit, study your lapidary catalogs carefully and compare the different features. Talk to a hobbyist who uses diamond equipment, or attend a lapidary show where dealers demonstrate diamond units.

DIAMOND WHEELS

When using diamond wheels for the first time, work slowly with a light pressure until you have a feel for the action of the wheels. Diamond is a hard, sharp abrasive and cuts faster and deeper than silicon carbide. It is easy to cut too deep, and if you should do this, you will have to recut or reshape the stone to a smaller size or make it with a low-domed top instead of a high-domed top.

The fine grit laps or discs are used more frequently by faceters. Many of the finer grits are available in syringe compounds and sprays or can be purchased in small plastic vials as loose grit or diamond bort. Remember that diamond wheels and discs must be used with a lubricant. Use the lubricant recommended by the manufacturer. Diamond powders are calibrated in micron sizes rather than grit sizes. To prevent contaminating your abrasives, particularly contaminating a finer abrasive with a coarse one, store the extra wheels, laps, and discs in plastic bags that close tightly. Always store them flat to prevent them from warping. Specially built cabinets with multiple shelves are available for storing wheels, laps, and discs.

PART THREE

SPECIAL LAPIDARY TECHNIQUES

6

LAPPING GEM MATERIALS

Lapping is a method of grinding and polishing the flat surfaces of intarsias, slabs, and geodes and for making bookends, clock faces, and trophy bases. Lap units were devised because it is difficult to obtain a completely flat surface on the face of a vertical grinding wheel, and the surfaces of horizontal grinding wheels or faceting laps are not large enough to flat-lap stones other than cabochons or small slabs. On an 8-inch-diameter (20.32 cm) lap, only 3 to 3½ inches (7.620 to 8.89 cm) of the lap surface is actually available for lapping, so any slab larger than 3 inches (7.620 cm) will not polish well on this size unit.

LAPPING UNITS

The first unit designed for lapping larger surfaces was a round cast iron lap, mounted horizontally, with a 3- to 4-inch (7.620 to 10.16 cm) rim around the lap plate. The lap is supported by a sturdy square stand or frame, with the lap itself mounted on a vertical arbor positioned in the center of the frame (Fig. 6-1). The motor is mounted on a cross-brace on the frame under the lap and connected to the arbor by a series of V-belts and pulleys.

Flat laps must be used with loose abrasives. The first grit used can be 80, 120, or 200. Before going to the 400 grit, thoroughly clean the lap and lap pan. This is necessary between each grit size used. The 600 grit will remove all scratches or sanding marks before the final polishing.

The smallest flat lap is a 10-inch-diameter (25.4 cm) bench model with 9-inch (22.86 cm) 100 and 200 grit grinding wheels that run horizontally. The bench model is also designed for 10-inch-diameter (25.4 cm) cast-aluminum sanding and polishing laps. Some lap units include more than one lap. You can also buy a 12-inch (30.48 cm) variable-speed or a 12-inch (30.48 cm) single-speed bench model. Floor stand lapping units are available with 16-inch (40.64 cm) or 18-inch (45.72 cm) laps.

A swing lap (Fig. 6-2) is especially adaptable for large, flat surfaces, since there is no arbor in the center of the base. The floor model will handle up to a 24-inch (60.96 cm) by 36-inch (91.44 cm) tabletop.

Swing laps are ideal for making intarsias and tabletops, particularly rect-

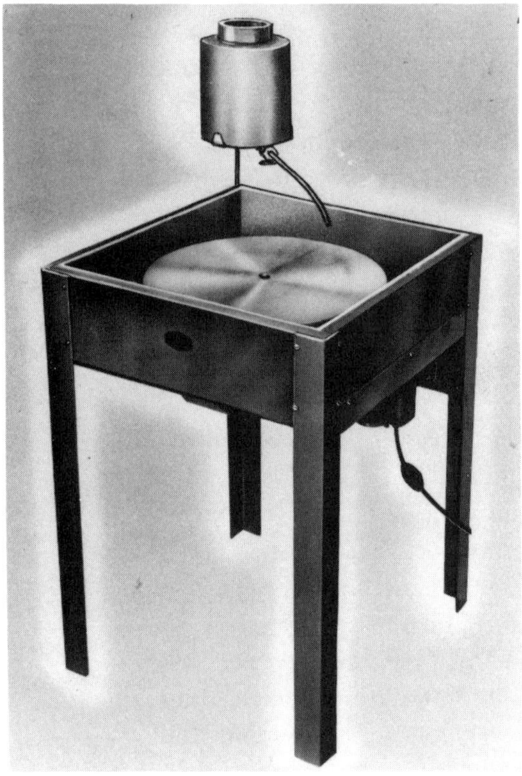

Fig. 6-1 A round cast-iron lap unit is excellent for lapping one piece at a time. You can make this type of lap yourself and adapt a sphere cup to fit. Courtesy, Covington Engineering Corp.

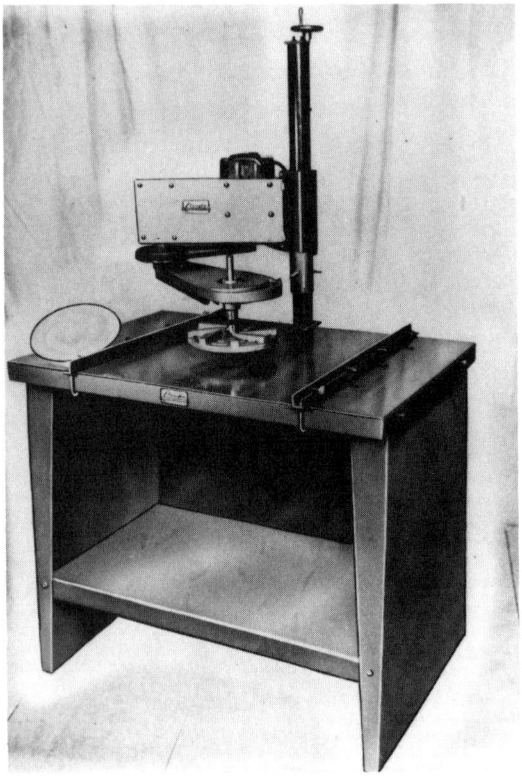

Fig. 6-2 A swing lap is convenient for lapping large areas such as intarsias and tabletops. The adjustable brackets on the table hold the rock firmly in place. Courtesy, Covington Engineering Corp.

angular tables, because the arm that holds the grinding and polishing heads is mounted on a sturdy upright shaft. The flex coupling on which the lap arm is mounted allows the lap to hug the work uniformly for smooth, fast lapping over the whole table surface. A manually operated lap grid head is mounted on the swing arm above the swing lap table. The lap grid heads are made of cast iron and are 8 inches (20.32 cm) in diameter. For polishing, you can use an 8-inch (20.32 cm) leather-covered aluminum polishing buff.

If you want to make your own lap unit, you can buy a stock horizontal running arbor and separate lap plates. Or you could make a unit from a flat lap kit, which is available with a 12-inch (30.28 cm) or 16-inch (40.44 cm) lap. Most lap units require a ½-horsepower, 110-volt, 60-cycle, vertical operating motor. If you buy a motor separately, make sure that it is compatible with the lap unit.

LAPPING GEODES AND SLABS

Flat slabs that are small in diameter can be embedded in a plaster of paris mold and all the slabs ground, sanded, and polished at the same time, if they are the same approximate hardness. To flat lap a group of slabs or geodes that have been cut in half, lay wax paper or plastic wrap on the swing lap table. Place the geodes close together, face down on the side that is to be polished, on top of the plastic wrap or wax paper. Make a frame to hold the plaster of paris. The frame should be just slightly higher than the thickest geode. Carefully pour the plaster of paris into the frame to barely cover the geodes. The plaster should be level and hold the geodes securely. Allow the plaster of paris to dry completely. Turn the block over and peel off the wax paper or plastic wrap. Then clamp the plaster block on the table of the swing lap. The swing lap table will accommodate a block of plaster up to 12 inches (30.48 cm) thick. Now you can grind, sand, and polish the entire block of geodes. Clean between each grind.

GRINDING AND POLISHING

Use 100 grit for the rough grind, 220 grit for the intermediate grind, 400 or 600 grit for the fine grind, and then the polishing powder. To lap semitransparent or transparent stone, you may need to use 1200 grit.

Mix the grit with just enough water for a good spreading consistency. Apply the abrasive to the lap with a 1-inch (2.54 cm) paint brush. If the lap becomes dry during grinding, the rock will grab or drag on the lap. When this happens, add more water to the abrasive. Some cast-iron laps have a water drip can mounted on the frame of the unit (see Fig. 6-1).

Keep your abrasives in small 8-ounce (275.304 ml) wide-mouthed jars with tight lids and mark the number of the grit size on each jar. Use a separate brush for each grit size and mark the brush handle with the grit size.

VIBRATING LAPS

Vibrating laps are a recent innovation, and they have become popular because it is not necessary to stand and hold the geodes or slabs by hand while grinding and polishing, and several pieces of rock can be worked at the same time. Some vibrating laps work on an oscillating principle (Fig. 6-3), while others

Fig. 6-3 With a vibrating lap you can lap more than one piece of rock at a time without having to hold each piece by hand. Courtesy, Lortone, Inc.

have a weight fitted to a sealed, adjustable ball-bearing unit that sets up the vibrating motion. The entire surface of the lap can be used because there is no arbor in the center of the lap plate. Vibrating laps are available in sizes from 10-inch (25.4 cm) to 20-inch (50.8 cm) lap plates. Before you buy a lapping unit, study lapidary catalogs and compare the features of each type of lap, and talk to other hobbyists.

To polish slabs or the faces of geodes that have been cut in half, you must put a bumper pad around the face of each geode half or around each slab so the edges will not chip when the objects bump each other. Because of difference in weight, do not mix slabs and geodes together. Some vibrating lap units come with bumper pads. If you buy a unit without bumper pads, you can make your own from strips of rubber or polyvinyl and wrap the strips around the edges of the geode or slab and secure the strips with masking tape. Some hobbyists cut bands from old inner tubes or strips of tread from old tires and tape them around the rock.

Always clean the bumper pads along with the laps and the slabs or geodes after each grinding stage. Clean the cavity of the geode thoroughly with a small brush to remove the accumulation of grit that gets into the hollows and crystal crevices. If you do not remove all the grit, it will scratch the surface of the geode face or slab. If that happens, you will have to start over again with the next coarser grit to remove the scratches before going on to the intermediate grinding, fine grinding, and polishing.

Check the geodes or slabs as you lap them to make sure they are being ground. If they are too lightweight, they will not grind properly. In this case you will have to make weights from hardwood blocks or end pieces of rock left from slabbing and place them on top of the slabs and secure them with dopping wax.

7

SPHERE AND BEAD MAKING AND DRILLING

SPHERE MAKING

Before the manufacture of sphere making units, hobbyists had to adapt their cast-iron lapping machines to sphere cutting by mounting a pair of sphere cups over the arbor of the lap. The cups are locked in place with a hexagonal nut or wing nut threaded to match the arbor threads. The grinding cups must be three-quarters the size of the finished sphere. Hobbyists either cut two lengths of pipe and grind or file the rough edges, slanting the inside edge about 45°, or use pipe nipples for the cutting cups because the edges are already round. A separate set of cups must be made for each sphere size. One cup locks in place on the lap arbor and the other is held by hand at an angle over the cup mounted on the lap.

Fortunately, with sphere making units now readily available, the job is much simplified.

Sphere Making Units

Most sphere making equipment is designed so that the arms holding the sphere cups are mounted at a slight angle. Sphere cups are available for cutting 2-inch (5.08 cm), 3-inch (7.62 cm), 5-inch (12.7 cm), 7-inch (17.78 cm), and 9-inch (22.86 cm) spheres.

A fully equipped machine usually includes one set of grit cups (usually in the buyer's choice of size), two polishing pads, two automatic grit pans, and a dual motor.

The automatic Little Sphere Maker will make tiny spheres ranging from ¼ inch (6.35 mm) to ⅞ inch (22.22 mm). It comes complete with one set of grit cups and polishing buffs.

Forming the Sphere

The first two stages in making a sphere are (1) to cut the rock into a perfect cube, and (2) to round off the corners of the cube to form an octahedron.

Wash the rough rock thoroughly and allow it to dry completely. Opaque rocks such as agate, jasper, and petrified wood must be free of any surface cracks because the cracks will be visible even after the stone is polished. Opaque transparent rocks should not only be fracture-free but have as few inclusions as possible. All inclusions and fractures in a transparent stone will show up clearly. Wear a head loupe or use a magnifying glass to check the stone for cracks and inclusions. The stone should be completely dry. If it is not, any cracks and inclusions will not be visible.

Cut the rock into a perfect cube. To form the cube into an octahedron, you will have to make a jig to hold the cube in the saw vise. To construct the jig, use a hardwood square block and cut a 90° V notch into the block. Place one corner of the cube in the notch of the jig and clamp the block and cube securely in the saw vise. Saw off the corner that is at right angles to the corner clamped in the notch. Rotate the cube in the jig until you have cut off all four corners. Continue to cut slant corners off both ends of the octahedron, making four cuts on each end. Grind the corners on the coarse grinding wheel until a roughly formed sphere emerges.

Always use a tool rest when grinding the corners. Holding the rock in your hand is awkward if you are making a sphere larger than 1½ inches (38.1 mm) in diameter. If you hold a large sphere to the grinding wheel without a tool rest, the wheel will bump the sphere and crack it. It can also ruin the grinding wheel.

Once the octahedron is nearly spherical, set it into the pipe cup of the sphere making unit (Fig. 7-1) or on the cup mounted in the center of the flat lap with a mixture of abrasive and water. For best results, the mixture should be a bit watery. If you use a lap unit with a pipe cup attached, place the cup on the top side of the rock at a 45° angle, not straight above. Move the pipe cup around to start the sphere turning. The sphere must turn constantly in all di-

Fig. 7-1 After the gem material has been cubed and rounded on a coarse grinding wheel, it is placed in the sphere cup of the sphere-making unit. Most machines can accommodate several sizes of sphere cups. Courtesy, Covington Engineering Corp.

rections while grinding in order to keep it round. Otherwise the finished sphere will be lopsided or will develop cutting marks.

Grinding the Sphere

The abrasives used for grinding spheres are similar to those used in lapping. Use 60/90 grit or 100 grit for the rough grind. The rough grind will round out the sphere and remove all the wheel marks, corners, and flat spots. To help keep the pipe cup supplied with grit while the sphere is being ground, many hobbyists line the sphere cup with strips of brown paper bags saturated with the grit mixture. When the sphere is round and symmetrical, clean everything thoroughly and proceed to the intermediate grind with 220 grit abrasive.

The intermediate grind should remove all the marks made by the coarse grit. Check the sphere and be sure that all of the scratches are gone and that the sphere has no flat spots. Once again, clean all the equipment and start the fine grind using 400 grit.

Most opaque gemstones should be ready for the polishing stage after the 400-grit fine grind. Transparent gemstones and some difficult-to-polish stones may require an additional fine grinding or prepolishing with 600 grit after the 400 grinding has been completed. To polish the sphere, clean everything thoroughly, then cover the sphere cups with either firm canvas or felt, leaving enough slack in the cover so the sphere will fit into the cup. Fasten the covers securely so that no loose strings can catch or become tangled. Mix the polish with water and apply it to the polishing cover in the cup. After polishing, check for imperfections and scratches. If any scratches show, you may have to repeat the fine grinding or, depending upon the depth of the scratches, regrind the sphere with either the 220 or the 400 grit.

Studio Visit: A Sphere Maker at Work

When William R. Dindinger of El Cajon, California, retired, he became interested in lapidary as a hobby. He built his own sphere making unit from the instructions in "Building a Three-Headed Sphere Machine" by J. B. Moore, published in the August 1979 *Lapidary Journal.* He soon became so interested in sphere making that he built a second unit, as well as a full set of grinding heads. To cut larger slabs than his 18-inch (45.72 cm) saw could accommodate, he built a 36-inch (91.44 cm) slab saw. After finishing this saw, he found that he needed a hoist to lift the large pieces of rough ornamental gem material onto the big saw. Bill built a 2,000-pound (907.84 kg) hoist to handle these large pieces.

Bill first exhibited his display in 1980. It showed the various steps in sphere grinding and polishing, and won "Best of Show." Bill also exhibited some clocks, but the judges disqualified them because the bases were not of the same material as the clock spheres.

Bill returned home and thought about how he could cut and polish the bases for the clock spheres. Cutting and polishing a square base presented no problem, but he wondered how he could hollow out a portion of the base to hold the clock sphere. After doing some research, Bill constructed a hollowing-out machine based on an idea taken from *Gem Cutting: A Lapidary's Manual*, by John Sinkankas. Now he could complete the bases, attaching them to the clock spheres with epoxy cement. Today, Bill continues to win ribbons and awards for his clocks.

Bill uses a 36-inch (91.44 cm) saw to cut the rough stone into 3- and 4-inch (7.62 and 10.16 cm) thick slabs and cubes (Fig. 7-2). He trims the corners on an 18-inch (45.72 cm) saw fitted with two jigs to hold the cube. The top jig holds one corner of the cube and the bottom jig holds the opposite corner firmly while the corresponding corners are trimmed off (see Fig. 7-2). He does the hand grinding and preforming on a 1½ by 8 inch (3.81 by 20.32 cm) 40 grit wheel. Bill uses a diamond wheel, rather than a silicon carbide one, because the diamond wheel cuts faster, stays round, and does not bounce or become bumpy. Bill built a hand rest to help steady the larger spheres during grinding and preforming.

Bill grinds the preformed sphere on his three-headed sphere machine,

Fig. 7-2 The cube is clamped in the hardwood jig mounted on an 18-inch (45.72 cm) saw. Courtesy, William R. Dindinger.

using 40/60 silicon carbide grit with cast-iron heads (pipe couplings) for the rough grind. He completes the intermediate grind with 240 silicon carbide grit and a plastic head set (PVC pipe couplings). He uses plastic pipe couplings with the finer grinds because the cast-iron heads tend to leave heavy scratches on the spheres. For his third and fourth grinds, Bill uses 400 and 600 silicon carbide grit and the plastic heads. He must clean everything thoroughly between each grind to prevent any of the coarser grit from scratching the sphere during the fine grind. To polish the sphere, he covers the plastic heads with leather, canvas, or felt and uses conventional polishes.

Bill makes the bases for his clock spheres by cutting and polishing a rectangular or square shape and hollowing it out with his hollow-grinding ma-

Fig. 7-3 The sawing stages in making a sphere. All cuts are made in opposites—first one side, then the other—to keep the sphere from getting out of round.

Fig. 7-4 The wheel grinding has six different stages.

Fig. 7-5 Sphere machine grinding stages, from left to right, using grit sizes: (1) 60, (2) 240, (3) 400, (4) 600, and (5) the final polish. Because of the different mineral content in marbles, a special mix of polishes is necessary. Tin and cerium oxides are mixed together and water added with a small amount of oxalic acid added last.

Fig. 7-6 Four polished spheres, left to right: Balerite marble, river marble, white marble, and another Balerite marble.

chine (Figs. 7-7 and 7-8). The basic housing of the unit is an open rectangular wooden frame with a motor mounted on top. The grinding disc, 8 inches (20.32 cm) by 3/8 to 3/4 inch (9.525 to 19.50 mm) thick, is attached to a shaft mounted on the lower platform of the housing and is connected to a large pulley at the back attached to the motor by a V-belt. A separate platform in front, holding the clock base, is attached to a separate shaft and operates independently of the grinding disc. It very slowly rotates the platform continuously.

Fig. 7-7 Bill made a diamond core drill the exact size he needed to drill out the area to receive the clock works (at left). It was drilled approximately 1¾ inches (44.45 mm) deep.

Fig. 7-9 The finished clock is 5¾ inches (14.605 cm) in diameter. The clock face is 3 inches (7.62 cm) in diameter.

The grinding wheel diameter on the hollow-grinding machine should be the same as the diameter of the sphere.

To display his finished spheres, Bill uses small plastic caster cups used under the legs of furniture to protect carpets. They are unobtrusive and the right depth and diameter to hold the finished spheres neatly in place.

BEAD MAKING

Before bead mills and bead-making units became available, the hobbyist had to make one bead at a time, using a process similar to sphere making. To hold the tiny spheres or beads, some hobbyists used bamboo rods. Because bamboo is hollow, the hobbyist could insert a tiny cube with the corners cut off

Fig. 7-8 (Opposite) Bill made this sphere-base grinding unit so he could hollow out the circle for inserting and cementing the sphere clock. Left to right: a finished sphere clock, the grinding unit (note the ring of modeling clay to hold the grit and water), the sphere clock that will be cemented to the hollowed-out base. Courtesy, William R. Dindinger.

Fig. 7-10 Most bead mills will grind more than one size of bead. Courtesy, Covington Engineering Corp.

into the end of the rod. With the help of a tool rest or hand rest placed in front of the grinding wheel, the bamboo stick could be moved gradually into the grinding wheel. The bamboo stick had to be held with both hands close to the end being guided against the wheel. The hobbyist's fingertips were used to guide the bead and keep it moving in a circular pattern to round off all the corners of the cube. Some hobbyists liked to have the bamboo stick long enough to go under the arm and braced it against the body for stability. Others made their bead-making cups from brass or aluminum tubing fastened to wooden doweling. This was a slow process and it became tedious and time-consuming when many beads were required.

Bead Mills

Today, several bead mills are available that will grind beads of various sizes. A 5-inch-diameter (12.5 cm) bead mill will grind approximately twenty ½-inch (12.7 mm) beads at one time. The same unit will also make up to ¾-inch (19.05 mm) beads. On these bead mills, however, only one size of bead can be made at one time. An 8-inch-diameter (20.32 cm) bead mill will make beads ranging up to 2 inches (50.8 mm) in diameter. Forty ½-inch (12.7 mm) beads can be ground at one time on this larger machine. The beads can be polished in a tumbler.

Beads can be faceted, round, oval, and baroque. Novelty shapes can be used as accents on a string of round beads. Beads can also be ground and polished in a tumbler.

Shaping the Beads

When using a bead mill, first cut the slabs of ornamental stone into strips of the same width as the thickness of the slabs so that the strips will be square. Then cut the square strips into sections the same length as the width and thickness to form small cubes. Grind off the corners of cubes on the grinding wheel before putting them into the bead mill.

The top and bottom plates of the bead mill have matching shallow round

Fig. 7-11 This bead mill will grind as many as 80 round 10 mm beads. Courtesy, Geode Industries, distributor for Imahashi Manufacturing Co., Ltd.

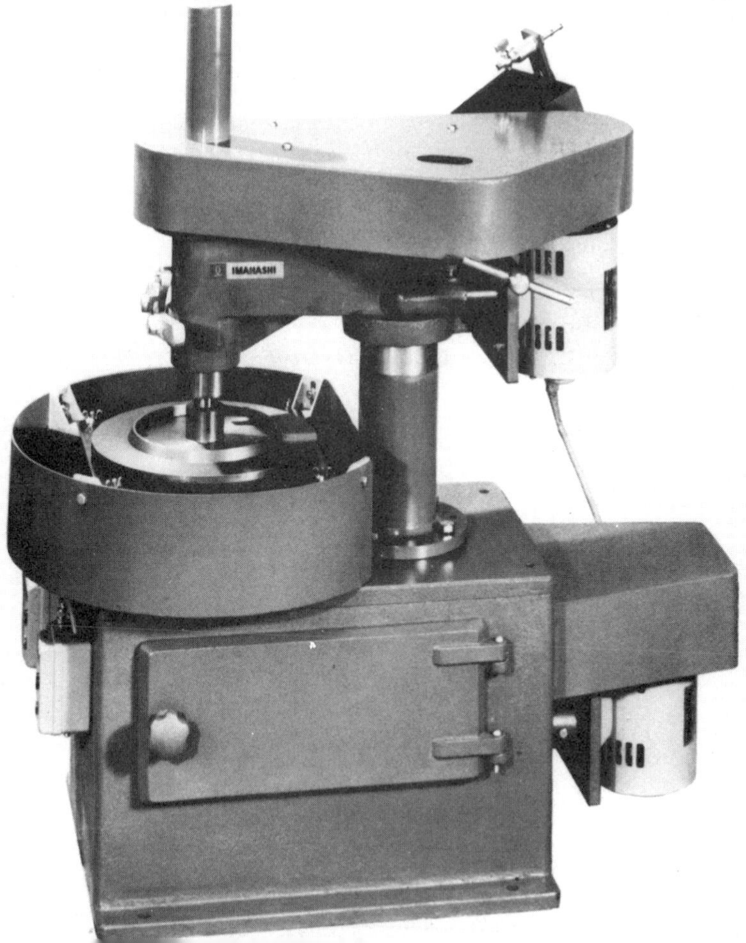

grooves that run in a circle around the arbor. Place the beads on the bottom plate, and add a thin mixture of abrasive and water to just cover the beads. The top plate is lowered onto the top of the semishaped beads and, when you turn on the motor, the beads will start rolling. Steady pressure must be exerted on the top plate to keep the beads rolling. As the beads start to grind down, add slightly more pressure to keep the beads rolling. When the beads become symmetrical, put them through the rough, intermediate, and fine grinds and polish them in a tumbler.

Elongated beads must be preformed on a trim saw and the sharp corners ground off on a grinding wheel before being tumbled in the rough, intermediate, and fine grinds, and then polished. The beads can be capped or notched and jump rings cemented into the notch. If the elongated beads are not too long, they can be drilled like the round beads.

DRILLING GEMSTONES

Drilling is a branch of lapidary that can work in conjunction with tumbling, bead making, and carving. You may want to drill a teardrop-shaped cabochon and attach a bail finding for a neck chain. The primary uses for drilling are for bead drilling, the insertion of findings, carving, and for cutting small inside curves on a variety of lapidary pieces.

GEOMETRIC BEADS

Geometric shaped beads which have angular corners are usually handmade or faceted. A slab of rock the thickness you want the beads to be can be cut into square strips, then flat lapped on a 10-inch horizontal lap and polished. After the strips are polished they can be cut into squares on a trim saw and the ends flat lapped and polished, then drilled.

Most of the angular or square beads, when examined very closely, have slightly rounder edges. Using a tumbler the strip of rock can be cut into squares and put into the tumbler and processed as you would for preforms.

In European countries, lapidaries often facet beads on automatic faceting machines. Other handmade bead forms are very often made in the Asian countries where labor is inexpensive.

The earliest form of drilling was with a bow-type drill. The drill point was usually a small tube drill or solid rod. The drills used today operate on a vibrating principle, which works well when very small holes are required, such as in beads or cabochons. Small tubing, sometimes as small as $\frac{1}{16}$ inch (1.587 mm) diameter, is used for fine bead holes. Steel, stainless steel, brass, or bronze tubing can be used. Lapidary supply stores that sell drills usually carry small diameter tubing. If you are not using an automatic vibrating drill, you must control the action of the drill by raising and lowering the drill bit to allow the water and the abrasive to flow into the hole being drilled. Always use a very light, even pressure. If you apply too much pressure and the bit remains in contact with the gemstone too long, too little abrasive will enter the hole and the drilling action will be impaired. This leads to friction-heat build-up and often the gemstone will break. This is not a worry with automatic drills.

Drill bits come in a variety of sizes and shapes. Be sure to select the proper size and type for your drill. Core drills in larger sizes are available for certain types of drills. Most of the larger sized core drills have the cutting edge embedded with diamond abrasive. All diamond drills, whether large or small, must have plenty of lubrication. Follow the instructions that come with the drill to achieve the best results. Small needle-type diamond drills can snap easily if you are not careful. If the drill breaks, you will have to replace the drill bit. Often when a small diamond drill breaks, the object being drilled will also break.

Drilling Beads

Use caution when drilling beads. Hold the bead securely or place it in a wooden jig. You can make a jig by placing a "V" notch in a block of wood and clamp the wood to the base of the drill. The bead can be held firmly in the "V" notch with beeswax or paraffin. The "V" notch should have a small hole drilled in the center, the same size as the drill bit being used. When you have drilled the bead approximately halfway through, stop the drill, remove the bead, and insert a small peg into the hole in the "V" notch. Turn the bead over and place the drilled hole on the peg to help center the bead in the "V" notch. Then, when you drill the bead from the opposite side, the two drill holes will meet in the center of the bead. The reason for turning the bead is to keep the opposite side of the drill hole from breaking out or chipping around the drill as it comes through the surface. Form a reservoir from child's clay or putty around the area where you are drilling. The reservoir will hold the water and abrasive under the drill bit while you drill.

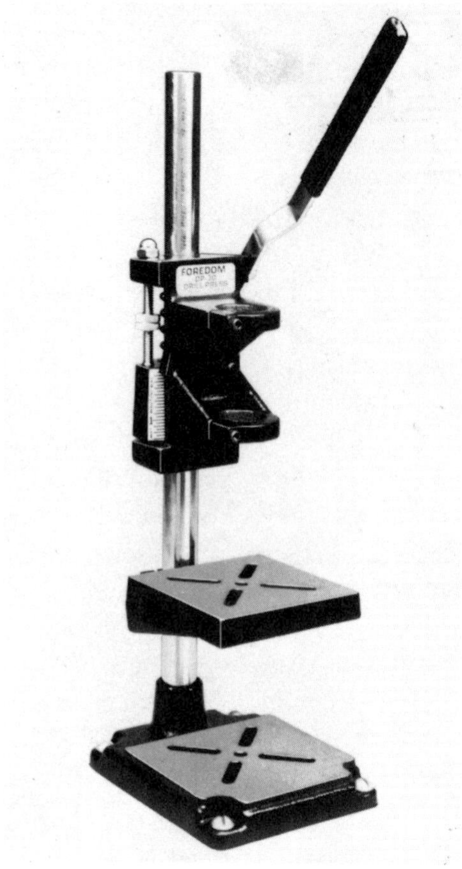

Fig. 7-12 To use a flex shaft for drilling with fine diamond drill bits, the flex shaft must be mounted in a drill stand. The drill must be held rigid to prevent the drill bit from breaking. Courtesy, Foredom Electric Company.

If you are drilling a cabochon or a flat slab or rock, fasten it to a flat board with beeswax, paraffin, or a small amount of dop wax to hold it solid. Clamp the board to the drill base and build the clay reservoir on the slab around the area to be drilled. The flat wooden base will also absorb the shock of the drill and keep the back of the cabochon or slab from chipping when the drill bit comes through. Some lapidary shops specialize in drilling, which comes in handy if you are drilling many beads.

Use water or a thin oil as a lubricant for drilling. When using a diamond core drill, follow the directions that come with the drill bits. Use loose silicon carbide abrasive in 100 or 120 grit with small tube drills. If the drill holes are extremely fine, use 400 grit. Some hobbyists prefer diamond abrasive drill bits because they cut faster. The grit sizes of diamond abrasives are comparable to those of silicon carbide abrasives. Loose diamond abrasive is seldom used.

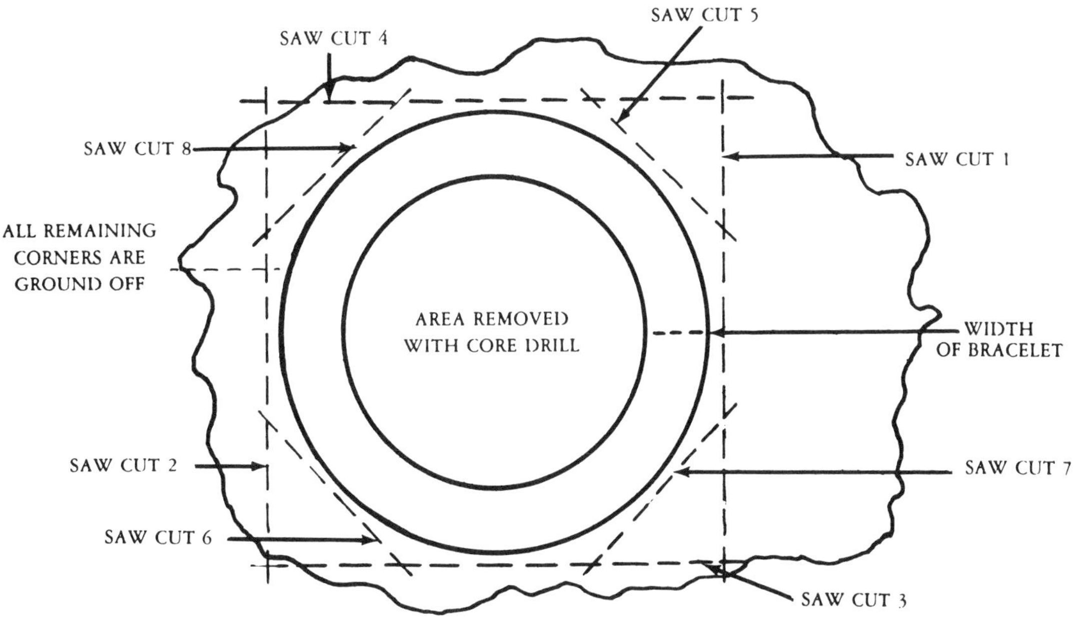

Fig. 7-13 Cutting diagram for making a bangle bracelet with a core drill. The dotted lines indicate the saw cuts that must be made before grinding off the corners. Illustration by Dara E. Yost.

MAKING BANGLE BRACELETS

The thickness of the slab will determine the thickness of the bracelet. The diameter of the drill should be large enough so that the bangle will slip easily over the hand and onto the wrist. If you use a core drill slightly smaller than the inside of the bracelet, you can sand it to the correct size. Do the sanding on a rubber-bonded abrasive wheel mounted on a tapered spindle or with a flex shaft.

1. Drill the inside of the bracelet and finish the inside. The outside material gives extra support while working the inside. Use diamond files and sanding cloth or rubber-bonded abrasives on a flex shaft.

2. Mark the outside circle of the bracelet with straight lines around the outside of the circle. These marks will show where to make the trim saw cuts to remove excess material from the outer edge of the bracelet.

3. Make the straight saw cuts and grind off all the corners left by the sawing operation on the grinding wheel.

4. Finish the bracelet by the usual process of sanding and polishing. Work carefully: the bracelet is fragile now.

Diamond Core Drills

Larger-size diamond core drills have a wide variety of uses in lapidary work, particularly in jewelry making (see Making Bangle Bracelets).

They are also useful for removing the centers of bowls or deep vases to be carved. If the top edge is flared, use the larger drill first to go as far as possible; then reduce the drill size to the next portion of the taper of the vase. A third drill may be necessary, perhaps a 1-inch (24.4 mm) core drill for the last cut. Then grind and sand the piece to smooth the areas between the cuts made by the different-size core drills.

Drills using fine drill tubing with silicon-carbide abrasives are handy for making small items. For gem materials that are 7 or less in hardness, you can use an empty ink cartridge from a ballpoint pen as the drill rod. For stones that are 8 or more in hardness, use a fine drill tubing, but with loose diamond abrasive rather than silicon carbide.

The drill rods of some fine diamond drills are embedded with bits of diamond or have a piece of diamond bort embedded in the end of the rod. Always use small, thin diamond points with care, and use plenty of water and a very light pressure to prevent the drill from overheating. Never force any diamond tool.

8

INLAY, MOSAICS, AND INTARSIAS

Inlay is the ancient art of placing a pattern of one material into another, such as a wooden box inlaid with a design of shell, ivory, or gemstone. Since antiquity, artisans of many cultures have inlaid small pieces of brilliantly colored glass or stone into hand-carved art objects, such as small decorative boxes, and chests and even furniture and musical instruments.

INLAY

Inlay is occasionally referred to as marquetry which is a technique of inlaying a decorative pattern onto a piece of wood. Small, detailed intarsias are inlaid into wooden or gemstone objects, such as decorative boxes or jewelry.

For example, squares of malachite can be inlayed in a geometric design and the design reversed or inlaid to run across the pattern.

The design is marked on the object and the sizes of the pieces to be inlaid are carefully marked and the areas scooped out for the inlay with carving tools. The materials used for inlay are shell, ivory, or gemstones. The designs are then cemented into the recessed areas. Miniature mosaics and mini-intarsias can also be inset into different jewelry pieces. Designs with butterflies, flowers or hearts can be inset into the base unit with the mini-mosaic or intarsia, rather than inlaid.

After making the intarsia, the pattern is scribed on the base and the base is cut through the center, both vertically and horizontally, and sectioned into four equal pieces. The four pieces are fitted, one at a time, to a section of the intarsia that will be in the center when the four base pieces are perfectly joined together again and are recemented into one solid piece. The whole piece is flat lapped, using the standard procedures of grinding, sanding, and polishing. The finished piece can be fashioned into a pendant or a bola tie.

MOSAICS

Many mosaics are stylized forms or patterns depicting fish, animals, trees, and other forms from nature. Some mosaic artists prefer to work with abstract patterns. Mosaic patterns and designs are endless, limited only by the imagination and ingenuity of the artist.

The best modern mosaics are made by two different methods. In one, the *tesserae* (small cubes of colored stones) are placed by hand on a wall or floor. The other method is to make an outline drawing on heavy paper that will represent in reverse, the full size of the design. The tesserae are glued in place on the paper, then the paper is cut into sections small enough to be handled easily and transferred to the surface prepared with special cement. The tesserae and paper are pressed together into cement. After the cement has set and become firm, the paper is carefully torn off and the joints in the cement are pointed with a metal hand tool.

In many modern mosaics the tesserae are often small glazed tiles, as in swimming pools, bathrooms, and kitchens. Many modern churches have been based on ancient Roman mosaics or combine Roman and medieval Italian mosaics.

Fine intricately patterned mosaics fitted together from hard stone are referred to as *piètre duré* or "Florentine mosaics." *Intarsias* have gradually evolved from basic mosaics into a somewhat different type because of the way the pieces are combined to form the picture and because of the backing. The intarsia pieces are cut and shaped to conform exactly to the pieces next to them, so that the pieces fit together perfectly, similar to a jigsaw puzzle. They are fitted so well that no cement shows in the joints.

For a floor mosaic, a cement foundation is laid by cement workers and the artist places the tesserae into the cement. The tesserae are usually small glazed or unglazed tiles or pieces broken off larger tiles. Sometimes both glazed and unglazed tiles are used in the same mosaic to achieve a desired effect. Various ornamental stones and gemstones are utilized for color and effect. Originally, small pieces were broken off with whatever tools were available, perhaps pliers or chisels and a hammer. Today, lapidaries use heavy pliers, called nippers, to break off small pieces of stone and then saw them to size.

Making a Wall Hanging

To make a mosaic wall hanging, you must make a plywood base to support the cement backing. If you are making the panel less than 2 feet (60.96 cm) square, use ½ inch (12.7 mm) plywood. On larger panels, use ¾ inch (19.05 mm) plywood. Plywood should be waterproofed so that it will not absorb moisture from the cement. Apply several coats of any good waterproofing lacquer or varnish. Marine plywood requires less preparation and fewer coats. Seal the edges of the plywood and place a thin metal strip around the outside. The strip should be slightly higher than the plywood base to prevent the cement from dripping over the edges. The stripping can be aluminum, brass, copper, or thin iron. Wax the stripping or cover it with wax paper or plastic wrapping paper so that you can remove it easily when the cement is dry. To hang the mosaic, put bolts through the plywood base with the screw threads extending beyond the back of the plywood.

A network of heavy mesh wire or metal lath is necessary to hold the cement and prevent cracks from developing in the mosaic after the cement has dried. The metal lath can be stretched from side to side across the plywood base. Depending on the size of the mosaic, the reinforced cement base can vary from ½ inch thick (12.7 mm) for small mosaics to 2 inches thick (50.8 mm) for larger panels.

While the cement is still pliable, point the joints with a round pointed tool. Wipe away any smeared cement on the tesserae with a damp cloth before it becomes too dry. You may have to scrape the cement from the edges of the tesserae with a palette knife.

To make a wall hanging or table, start with ¾-inch (19.05 mm) plywood. Work out the pattern on a piece of heavy paper the same size as the finished mosaic; then transfer the pattern to the plywood base. Prepare the rocks or gem materials if you have not already done so. Since a mosaic may require as many as 1,000 or 2,000 stones, depending on its size, you may want to purchase already tumbled stones or polished slabs.

If you are using polished slabs, trim them to size and shape on a trim saw

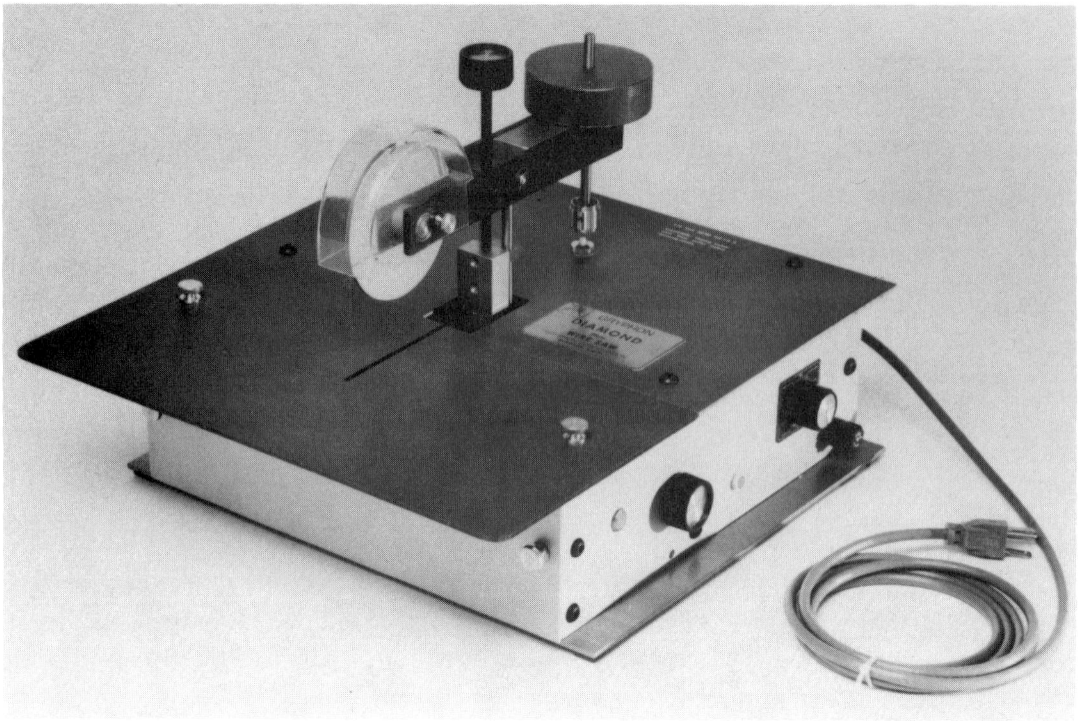

Fig. 8-1 A diamond wire saw will save time when cutting intricate curves for intarsia. Courtesy, Gryphon Corp.

and smooth the edges by the regular methods of grinding, sanding, and polishing. The stone pieces are cemented to the plywood base with an epoxy cement. All slabs should be 3⁄16 inch thick (14.2875 mm). The pieces should be glued close enough together so that there is no opening larger than 1⁄4 inch (6.35 mm), and smaller if at all possible. Allow the panel or tabletop to dry thoroughly, at least twenty-four hours.

Grouting the Stones

All areas in between the stones must be filled with grout. Grout powder can be purchased in hobby shops that specialize in mosaic supplies or in hardware stores. The powder is white, but can be tinted with dye or paint pigment. To mix the grout, slowly add water until the grout is about the consistency of thick whipping cream. The grout will be poured over the entire surface and forced into the crevices and low areas. When the grout has set for about an hour but is still slightly damp, wipe the stone surface with a damp sponge and scrape away excess grout on the stones with a small pick or palette knife. This is time-consuming, but if you don't do this, the finished mosaic will appear fuzzy. Clean the mosaic before the grout gets too dry. After cleaning the mosaic, brush it with a soft clean paint brush and buff with a soft cloth.

Some hobbyists prefer to use epoxy resins or fiberglass resins for mosaic tabletops so that the tables will be considerably lighter in weight than with the standard cement backings. If you use resins, you must polish the stones or slabs before you begin. To mix the resin, follow the instructions on the container. Epoxy resins can be purchased from hobby supply stores.

Prepare the table surface by placing a waxed stripping around the outside edge of the tabletop. When the tabletop has hardened, remove the stripping and finish the edges by hand.

INTARSIAS

A number of lapidary hobbyists specialize in intarsias. We will visit the workshops of two such artisans in this section, to see their work and learn their problem-solving approaches.

Studio Visit: A Landscape Artist

William Grundke, an intarsia artist, specializes in landscapes and country and street scenes (see color Figs. 22 and 23). Most of his pictures are approximately 14 by 16 inches (35.56 by 40.64 cm) or 12 by 14 inches (30.48 by 35.56 cm). Bill paints or sketches the picture and then makes a paper pattern, numbering the various parts of the intarsia. He makes several copies of the pattern in case he over- or undercuts a stone piece and has to start again.

Next, Bill selects the colors of the slabs that will complement the intarsia. If a slab contains a pattern, he puts it aside until he finds the perfect spot for it. To ensure that he has enough slabs of one color, perhaps for a barn or farmhouse made from petrified wood, he cuts multiple slabs from one piece of rough so they will match. He often starts with slabs ¼ inch thick (6.35 mm), since his method of making intarsias requires considerable lapping.

If Bill thinks he cannot obtain enough slabs from one piece of rough material, he will slab the rough thinner and, if necessary, back it with another

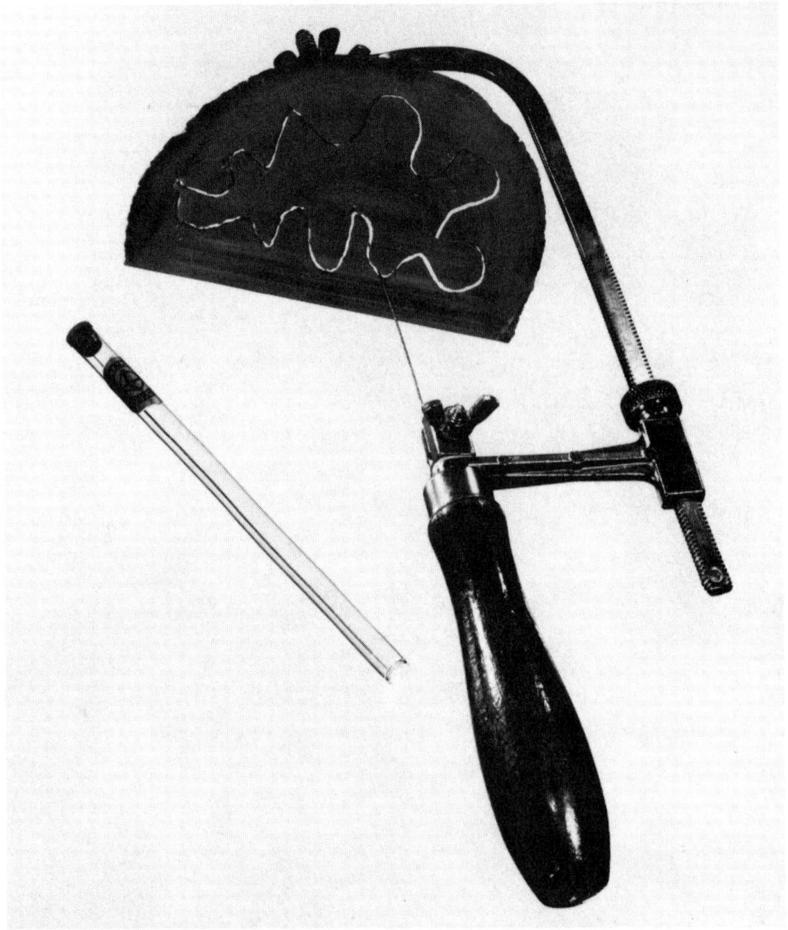

Fig. 8-2 Intarsia pieces with fine detail can be cut with a fine diamond-wire saw blade as shown here. You can also use a jeweler's saw frame and a medium saw blade with silicon-carbide grit and water. Courtesy, Crystalite Corporation.

type of gem material, making a doublet. When Bill needs thin, straight strips, he uses a jeweler's saw frame with a 2/0 saw blade with silicon carbide grit and water (see Fig. 8-2). This is how he cut the strips to form the barn boards in the intarsia shown in Figure 8-4. He cut the strips absolutely straight and parallel from ⅛ to $^{3}/_{16}$ inch (3.175 to 4.762 mm) wide, but he varied the widths of the strips to enhance the realism of the barn.

Bill works in small units and then joins one unit to the other. To combine the units, he made his own frame and press with a ½-inch (12.7 mm) plyboard work surface to which he cemented ⅛-inch (3.175 mm) Masonite. Across the top and down one intersecting edge, he placed 1-inch-wide (25.4 mm) oak strips ¼ inch (6.35 mm) thick. When he combines two units or pieces of one

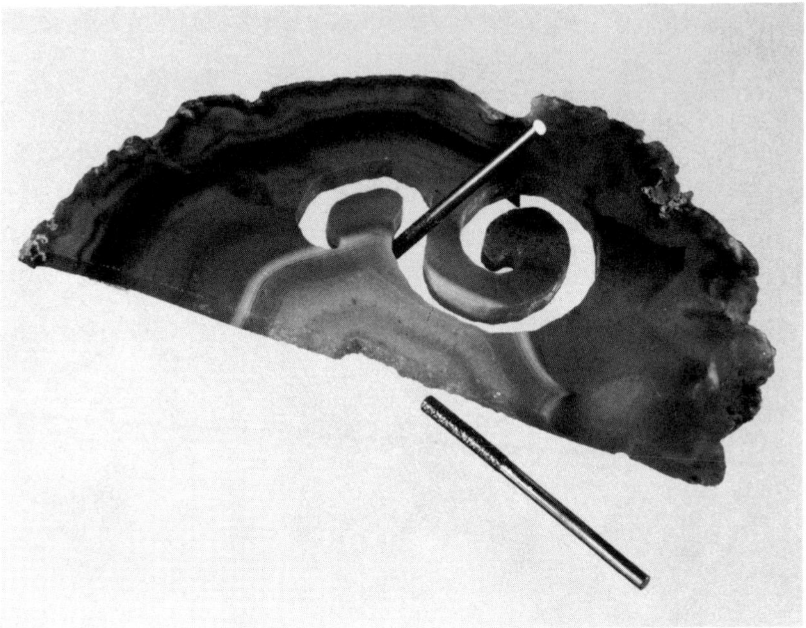

Fig. 8-3 A diamond router is ideal for smoothing tight inside curves. Courtesy, Crystalite Corporation.

unit, he butts them against the two oak strips and secures them with aluminum push pins. He also devised press bars to hold the units in place and keep them from warping the intarsia as the units dry. Bill places two sheets of wax paper under the units so the cement will not stick to the Masonite.

Bill uses Epoxy 220 because it dries slowly enough to allow him to get a tight fit between pieces. He uses Epoxy 330 as in Figure 8-5 on snow scenes because it does not yellow as much as Epoxy 220. He also uses colored epoxy to make joins less obvious. Polyester resin pigments can be purchased at hobby or craft stores. Bill also colors his cement by grinding small chips of natural gem materials into a fine powder, then mixing the powder with the epoxy and letting it flow into the tiny areas. Coloring the epoxy with ground gemstone gives the intarsia a more realistic appearance, as in the barn boards, which he colored with finely ground black and brown gemstones.

When the cement on one unit is thoroughly dry, Bill laps the unit before going on to the next one. He uses 220 silicon carbide grit for gemstones of the same hardness. For stones of different hardness, he uses 400 grit so the softer material will not undercut. Once Bill has cemented all the units together, he trims the outside edges, making sure all corners form a 90° angle. To prevent chipping the corners, he stops the trim cut almost at the corner instead of

Fig. 8-4 *Tranquillity*, an intarsia by William Grundke. Bill cut all of the straight strips of petrified wood for the barns with a jeweler's saw and a No. 2/0 saw blade with silicon carbide and water. Courtesy, William E. Grundke.

Fig. 8-5 *Maria Gern* by William Grundke. Bill used howlite for the snow because it is pure white with black veining, which simulates cracks in the snow. Courtesy, William E. Grundke.

completing the cut to the end. He then turns the finished intarsia around and cuts from the corner in to meet the first cut.

After trimming and smoothing the outside edges, Bill mounts a brass stripping, $\frac{1}{16}$ inch thick (1.587 mm) and $\frac{5}{16}$ inch wide (7.9375 mm), on all four sides, and miters the corners for an exact fit. The brass stripping must be clean or the epoxy will not adhere. Bill cleans the stripping with a Mizzy wheel, then scrapes off any cement on the picture with a palette knife. Next, he flat-laps the whole picture, starting with 220 grit for the coarse grind and continuing through the intermediate grind to the 600-grit fine grind. Often Bill prefers a semigloss finish rather than a high polish, and to achieve this he often finishes the sanding with a worn-out 600-grit sanding belt, working it by hand.

Bill mounts his intarsias for framing, using flat headed bolts (machine screws) with hexagonal nuts. He grinds one edge of each bolt flat to keep it from turning in the epoxy. Then he embeds the bolts in plastic steel epoxy in each corner of the intarsia. If the heads of the bolts extend beyond the brass stripping, they must be countersunk. Bill cuts a piece of Masonite, allowing a border around the intarsia, and drills the holes for the bolts. He covers the Masonite with velvet, choosing a color to compliment the intarsia, and sprays several coats of 3M Spray Adhesive on the back of the velvet and on the smooth side of the Masonite. When the velvet and the Masonite are joined, the cement acts like contact paper.

Bill uses a wide-bristle paint brush to remove the wrinkles in the velvet. He then trims the excess velvet with a sharp knife, cuts the bolt holes through the velvet, fastens the intarsia to the Masonite, and frames the picture. Bill Grundke's intarsias have been exhibited at many shows (see color Figs. 22 and 23).

Studio Visit: Creating *Piètre Duré*

Olive Colhour is particularly interested in Florentine *piètre duré*. During her research, she found that sculptured mosaics were somewhat rare and that few remain in existence today. One of her earlier *piètre duré* intarsias, entitled *Gypsy Rhythm*, 18 by 24 inches (45.72 by 60.96 cm), is comprised of five hundred pieces of gemstone carved in relief (see color Fig. 19).Olive carved and polished each piece individually before she assembled all the pieces.

Since Olive exhibits in gem and mineral shows all over the country and in Europe, she has started to use the new epoxy cements and plastic resins because they reduce the weight of the intarsia. She hangs all of her intarsias, using an ⅛-inch-thick (3.175 mm) sheet of aluminum that she fits at the top edge with hangers so the finished intarsia hangs from the backing rather than from the frame.

Olive often starts with an original drawing, as in her *El Picaro (The Rascal)*, based on Pancho Villa (see Figs. 8-6 and 8-7). She selected the brightest colors from her stock of gemstones for the sombrero and serape. She used shaded pieces of Bruneau Canyon jasper to simulate the skin tones. (See color Fig. 20).

For skin tones, which often require an exact match of stones, Olive slabs one piece of rough rock into several slices. Olive marks areas for the joins that are the least obvious and selects and modifies the lines of the shadows and the sketched-in lines of the facial features, such as the cheekbones, the contour lines of the face, chin, hairline, eyes, the eyebrows, and the muscle lines of a smile. She tries to use curved lines rather than straight lines and as few joins as possible, since they will define and separate the segments on her master plan. She makes several copies of her tracings from the master copy and numbers the segments so that she can easily identify them when they are cut apart.

With a sharp stencil knife, Olive cuts one pattern apart in the same manner as a jigsaw puzzle. At this stage she may decide to eliminate a piece or cut another piece into two parts. She arranges the pieces of gemstone until she has the proper tone or color, then glues the cutout paper pattern to the gemstone slab. When the cement is dry, she paints the piece with clear shellac and cuts away the unwanted sections of the slab with a trim saw.

Olive uses three different grinding wheels ½ inch wide (12.7 mm) by 6 inches (15.24 cm) in diameter. One wheel is dressed for grinding deep curves, another for grinding shallow curves, and the third is dressed flat for grinding straight lines. If a curve is too sharp or an area too small for the grinding wheels, she uses a flex shaft with a variety of small tools and points. She usually grinds a slight bevel on the edges of the pieces to allow for the epoxy when she cements the pieces together. While fitting the pieces together, she may discover a flaw in the stone that was not noticeable before, or the color may not match exactly. If she has to remake a piece, she cuts apart another copy of her drawing to use as the pattern.

Once she has ground several pieces to fit, Olive places them on a rolled-out piece of child's clay to hold them in place until she has fitted several more pieces together perfectly into a unit. She then removes them from the clay and cleans them thoroughly in lacquer thinner. Now she is ready to cement them together. She puts the pieces face down on a heavy piece of plate glass covered with a tightly fitted sheet of polyethylene plastic to keep the epoxy from sticking to the glass. The epoxy takes about 24 hours to dry. A heat lamp will speed the drying, but the pieces must be weighted or taped down or the outer edges may lift up and warp.

When all of the small units have been completed, Olive fits one segment or unit to the next one in the same way she fits the single pieces into a unit. Olive cuts all the slices of rock ⅛ inch thick (3.175 mm), plus or minus 10 thousandths of an inch (.00254 mm), using a micrometer. She does this so that when the pieces are glued together there will be few spaces on the back of the intarsia to be filled with epoxy. If there is any variation in thickness, she fills the space with plastic aluminum.

After the epoxy cement is thoroughly dry, she scores the ⅛-inch (3.175

Fig. 8-6 Olive Colhour places cut and numbered pieces of rock onto her master diagram for her intarsia *El Picaro* (The Rascal) to see if they match properly. Courtesy, Olive M. Colhour and the Lapidary Journal, Inc.

Fig. 8-7 Olive matches the color of the rock to the color in her painting before starting the intarsia. Courtesy, Olive M. Colhour and the Lapidary Journal, Inc.

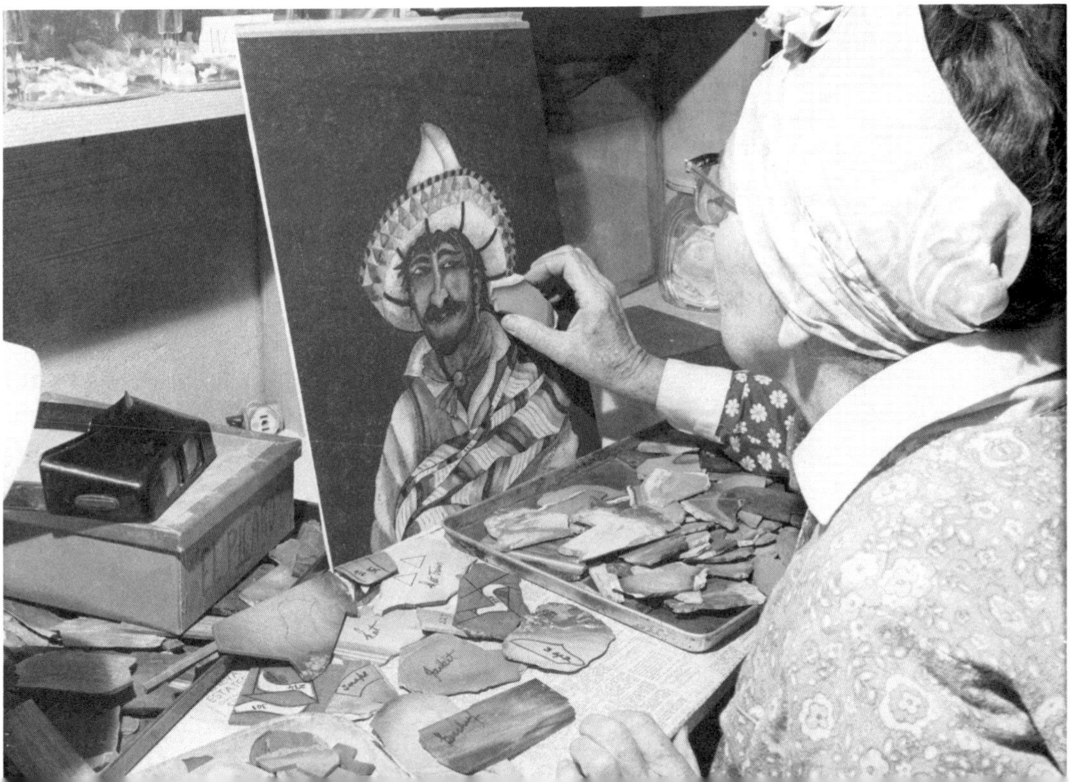

mm) sheet aluminum on the glue side and cements the intarsia to the scored side of the backing with epoxy. She tapes around the entire edge of the backing so that the epoxy will not flow out while it is drying.

To polish the intarsia, Olive pours a level layer of plaster of paris around it to keep it secure. She uses a flat lapping unit to finish the pieces, using the regular grinding, sanding, and polishing methods.

In *El Picaro*, Olive used jasper, black jade, agate, lapis lazuli, rhyolite, chrysoprase, wonderstone, aventurine, agatized wood, and crystallized hornblende for the black background (see color Fig. 20).

Some of Olive's other intarsias include *African Belle*, which took her three months to complete and is comprised of 100 pieces of gem materials. Her *Geisha* contains 154 pieces of 14 different materials and required 436 hours to complete. *Fringed Lily* was made of abalone shell and jade and took approximately 300 hours. She has also completed a portrait of Sir Winston Churchill, comprised of approximately 465 pieces of gemstone material. It took Olive almost three years to complete this lifelike intarsia portrait.

Olive's latest intarsia, a true Florentine mosaic, portrays Olive's hands and is entitled *These Are Mine* (see color Fig. 21). The background of the intarsia includes an open Bible, a plate of bread, a closed book, some pearls, and a glass of water. The intarsia measures 16 by 20 inches (40.64 by 50.8 cm) and required more then 1,800 hours to complete. Each section was an individual project in itself. Olive started with the closed book, using black jade for the lettering, pieces of claystone from Texas for the cover, red jasper for the trim, red wonderstone and ruby culet (red colored glass) for the highlights and shadows on the curve of the binding. The edges are white agate and jasper, the shadows are gray wonderstone, and the bottom of the book is Washington petrified wood.

Olive made the pearls from abalone shell, with a background of brucite. The bread was made from Bruneau jasper. For the plate she used a wide variety of colorful pink rhodonite, black jade, lavender jasper, green andesite, and white chert. The sleeves on her arms are gray and white chert and the cufflinks are abalone shell.

Olive made the hands from a piece of Canadian rhodonite that had a freckled appearance, blended with various shades of rose, gray, and white that blended with the open pages of the Bible, and the same material which had a moss-like appearance for her hands. Olive tried several jaspers, but none had the blotchy appearance that she needed. The material was so fractured that she had to reinforce it with epoxy cement before cutting and polishing. The cement had to be removed from both sides before fitting it to the rest of the unit.

After combining all the sections, Olive finished the surface by hand, using her optical lap. The lapping itself took almost twenty hours.

A Survey of Other Intarsia Methods

The late Joseph A. Phetteplace, owner of the Phetteplace Inlay Company, was an early leader in the field of modern intarsia making. He did most of his work in shell inlay, but one of his most famous *piètre duré* pieces, *Man O' War*, was done in hard stone—tigereye, jade, peristerite, and malchite—and contains more then 1,000 individual pieces. The intarsia, 2 by 3 feet (0.6096 by 0.9144 m), cost well over two thousand dollars and took more then 3,000 hours to complete.

Joe's life-size portrayal of President Lincoln was probably his most famous portrait. It weighs 125 pounds (56.699 kg) and required 2,700 pieces of gemstone materials. His large portrait of Lincoln convinced him that he could do portraits in miniature as well. He started a series of Presidents in Miniature, and at the time of the Bicentennial he had completed four miniatures.

The oval miniatures each measured 1¾ by 2¾ inches (44.45 by 68.85 mm). Each was matted and mounted in a handmade walnut frame, 6½ inches high (16.51 cm) by 6 inches wide (15.26 cm), with an engraved bronze nameplate.

Joe used mostly shell for the miniatures—mother-of-pearl, red-brown mother-of-pearl from the Indian Ocean, black coral from Hawaii, jet from England, ivory from Africa, and red and orange coral and black mother-of-pearl from Tahiti. When he was working on the miniatures, some of the materials were becoming hard to get and some had become unobtainable.

He often had to discard pieces after they had been cut and fitted because the color was wrong or the piece was flawed. He paid particular attention to the smallest details and worked from the best photographs he could obtain. Although he used several different cements, no cement was visible on the finished miniatures, even under magnification. Joe finished six miniatures before he died: George Washington, James Madison, Theodore Roosevelt, Thomas Jefferson, John Adams, and Abraham Lincoln.

In addition to *Lincoln* and *Man O' War*, Joe's large intarsias included a 10,000-piece picture of a panorama of the Century of Progress Exposition in Chicago, which took 2,600 hours to complete, and a replica of the Official

Symbol of Apollo II. Joe also did a number of bird miniatures and many inlay jewelry pieces.

Another interesting possibility is making a three-dimensional intarsia. These are usually much like the sculptured intarsia described earlier, the main difference being that not all pieces are sculptured. Most of the pieces are flat, with the exception of the parts which would be fully round on a real building, such as the domes on churches, capitol buildings, or mosques.

Cutting individual pieces can be accomplished in the usual manner. But when the pieces are cemented to each other, instead of cementing each piece flush, side by side, the pieces must overlap, with one edge *under* the one to which it is being cemented. This must be considered when trimming the slabs.

Studio Visit: Making Pictures of Crushed Stone

Crushed stone pictures have a three-dimensional quality which can be achieved by applying several layers of finely crushed gem material on top of each other, then cementing it to a Masonite backing with white glue. The de-

BIRD INTARSIAS

Bird intarsias demand an exacting choice of materials in order to simulate the intricate feather patterns. Some hobbyists work with the patterns face down on a piece of wax-coated glass. Another method is working on a $^3/_{16}$-inch-thick (4.7625 mm) piece of Plexiglas. The Plexiglas must be lightly sanded so that the epoxy resins will hold securely. The intarsia is worked face up so that each piece can be perfectly fitted and any imperfection or incorrect coloring of a piece immediately detected. A thin part or a slender line can be finished on one side and then cemented to the corresponding piece. After the cemented area has dried, the two pieces can be held so that the thin piece, which has the added strength of the joined piece, can be ground as thin as necessary from the opposite side of the join. All slabs should be cut as close to the same thickness as possible so that the entire cemented piece will be smooth.

Small units of six to eight pieces are completed separately, then fitted to the larger unit. The most intricate areas close to the center of the intarsia should be done first. When the intarsia is finished and the cement is dry, the whole picture is lapped smooth and level, starting with 200 grit and progressing to 400 and 600 grit. Either cerium oxide or tin oxide can be used to polish the intarsia.

sign is sketched on Masonite and glue applied to one area at a time, pressing the finely crushed rock into the glue. The area is allowed to dry, and the loose aggregate is shaken off the picture.

Daisie B. Skidmore specializes in small landscapes, 12 by 16 inches (30.48 by 40.64 cm), and pictures of animals and birds in natural settings. Daisie uses artist's canvas glued to a fiberboard backing so that the canvas will not buckle. Instead of using crushed rock, Daisie uses tiny tumbled stones, usually in the zero size, which measures approximately ⅛ inch (3.175 mm). She orders most of her stones from a Western supplier who sells graded sizes in all colors.

Daisie sketches the design on the artist's canvas and follows the basic sketch, occasionally making slight changes whenever she thinks they will improve the design. She cements the tumbled stones to the canvas with white glue applied from a small squeeze bottle through a shortened hypodermic needle fitted in at the neck to allow just enough glue to cement one stone. She places each stone into the glue and then onto the canvas. Occasionally, Daisie will use an unpolished stone for a special effect. One of Daisie's pictures requires approximately 20,000 tumbled stones. Since the stones are already polished, she does not have to repolish them.

When the picture is dry, Daisie brushes it with a soft housepainting brush to remove any lint of dust. To bring up the luster of the tumbled stones, she buffs the picture with a soft cloth. To clean the picture from time to time, Daisie sprays it lightly with Windex or ammonia water and blots the picture immediately to absorb excess moisture in the crevices. She then brushes and buffs the picture to bring out the vibrance of the colors.

9

GEM CARVING

Gem carving has a long and ancient history. The beginning of carving or engraving in the Orient can be dated to the early Chow Dynasty (1122–49 B.C.) in China. In ancient Egypt, artisan-craftsman worked with steatite (massive talc) and colored quartzes such as amethyst, carnelian, and jasper. The Romans carved scarabs and stones of carnelian, jasper, and sapphire and made cameos from agate and shell.

During the Middle Ages, Idar-Oberstein, in the Valley of Nahe, Germany, became a gem-carving center because of the wealth of agates and other gemstones found in the mountains nearby. One of the earliest records date the beginning of the gem cutting industry in Idar-Oberstein to 1454. Artisans built small one-story structures on the banks of the Idarbach (Idar River) and powered their large sandstone wheels, which weighed nearly 4,000 pounds (1814.369 kg), with waterwheels operated by water from the river. The gem cutters lay stretched out on their stomachs on benches mounted in front of the wheels and pressed the stones against the face of the sandstone wheels. Houses were built close together so that two families could share a waterwheel.

A family in Idar-Oberstein considered itself prosperous if it owned a sandstone wheel. If a cutter had two sons, one inherited the right-hand side of the wheel and the other son inherited the left-hand side. Much later, when electricity was brought in, the artisans moved further up the valley sides and established the cutting centers that are still famous today.

Fig. 9-1 The cutting shops along the Nahe River in old Idar-Oberstein were built close together so that two shops could share a waterwheel. Photograph by G. Presser. Courtesy, Harold and Erica Van Pelt Photographers.

The cutters received a Guild Charter in 1603, and only the sons of the master cutters were eligible to join. In the seventeenth century, the agate drillers received their own charter. The industry prospered until 1800, when the agate and jasper deposits in the nearby mountains became depleted. The craftsmen imported agates and jaspers from India and bought amethyst and rock crystal from Switzerland, but they could not obtain enough to keep all the carving plants busy.

Some of the cutters went back to farming. Many of the younger people emigrated to Brazil or went to Paris to learn the art of cameo cutting. Some of the cutters who had emigrated to Brazil started shipping agates home to Idar-Oberstein and the cutting plants were reopened. In the meantime, the technique of sawing stones was introduced.

The young cameo cutters returned from Paris and set up their own carving shops, which flourished. In 1875, an itinerant artisan introduced the art of cutting hard stone on a metal lap (the beginning of faceting), which he had learned in Bohemia. The cutting was originally done with emery and later with corundum. The artisans of Idar-Oberstein now needed new stones that could be cut on the metal lap, so they began to import rubies, sapphires, and garnets

Fig. 9-2 This shop in early Idar-Oberstein was later converted to electricity. Note the big sandstone wheel stored in the left rear corner of the shop and the large saw in the front. Photograph by Harold and Erica Van Pelt Photographers.

Fig. 9-3 Cutting and polishing a flat slice of agate on a large sandstone wheel in Idar-Oberstein. Photograph by Harold and Erica Van Pelt Photographers.

Fig. 9-4 All the wheels in one shop in Idar-Oberstein ran off of a jack shaft turned by wide, flat belts. Photograph by Harold and Erica Van Pelt Photographers.

Fig. 9-5 In Idar-Oberstein, the large wheels, turned by the wide flat belts, weighed about 4,000 pounds (1814.36 kg). Photograph by Harold and Erica Van Pelt Photographers.

from India, tigereye from South Africa, moonstone from Ceylon (Sri Lanka), and nephrite jade from New Zealand.

In 1886, the first diamond-cutting shop was opened, and gem merchants who had learned pearl cutting in Paris introduced the craft as well. The Idar-Oberstein merchants now had sufficient knowledge to produce a full range of gem materials by various cutting methods. The apprenticeship system continued to survive, with fathers teaching the trade to their sons.

Gem cutting was halted during World War I, but after the war the industry was revived and new methods were introduced using steam and electricity. Some of the old buildings have been modernized and today many of the carving shops are now operated by third- and fourth-generation families.

The early Chinese became masters at carving nephrite jade from Chinese Turkistan before jadeite was discovered in Burma during the eighteenth century. Some of the large fine carvings required more than one generation to complete. The master Chinese carvers also established an apprenticeship sys-

Fig. 9-6 In the same cutting shop in Idar-Oberstein, a worker prepares to cut the edge off a large rock. Photograph by Harold and Erica Van Pelt Photographers.

tem where a number of carvers could work on a single carving on a production line. When the communists took over mainland China, many carvers fled to Taiwan and Hong Kong and reestablished their shops, which continue to flourish.

CARVING GEMSTONES

Carving gemstones does not require formal training, but it does require a sense of balance, proportion, and color, as well as a great deal of patience. A knowledge of the basic skills of sawing, grinding, sanding, and polishing are essential, and a good reference book is helpful. To begin, all you need are

Fig. 9-7 Hing Wa Lee puts some finishing touches on a jadeite urn with his flex shaft. Photograph by Claire Curran.

CARVING IN THE CHINESE TRADITION

Hing Wa Lee, a Chinese carver who emigrated to the United States, settling on the east coast and later moving to Los Angeles, established a business and began teaching carving classes. He now carves commissioned pieces and repairs damaged carvings.

Hing Wa learned to carve by the traditional Chinese method of using a fixed shaft with a foot treadle and emery abrasives. Although he still uses his fixed shaft method, he now uses a flex shaft as well and makes many of his own tools.

Hing Wa's designs, whether for large or small pieces such as ivory netsuke, beads, pendants, and small figures, all have graceful, delicate lines. He carves in nephrite and jadeite (see color Fig. 25), and is always looking for new, unusual materials, such as sugilite (see color Fig. 24). He buys the best material he can and encourages his students to do so as well. He also makes carvings from quartz gems, opal, turquoise, tourmaline, amber, and ivory.

Fig. 9-8 The Possum by Dale Blankenship, an example of carving in the round.

Fig. 9-9 Small carvings such as this flower can be easily accomplished with a flex shaft and small diamond tools, Here, a Flexodisc diamond tool is being used to round the inside edges of the flower. Courtesy, Crystalite Corporation.

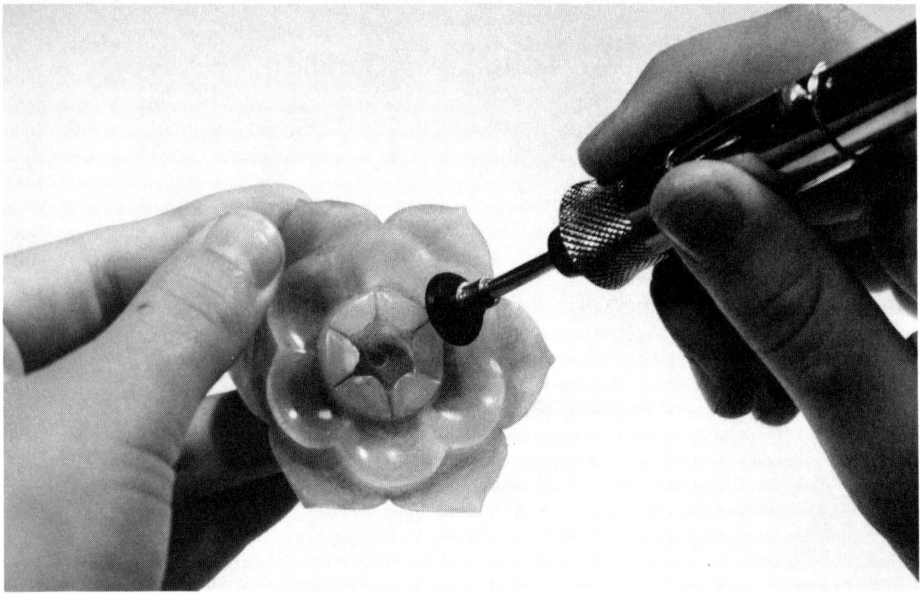

some soft materials, such as soapstone, ivory, alabaster, amber, and travertine onyx, and a few simple hand tools, such as a sharp knife, a 2/0-cut file and a finer file, sanding boards or sand cloth, and a cotton flannel polishing buff or a leather polishing disc.

There are several main types of carving: relief carving, carving in the round, and composite or assembled carving. In a relief carving, the design is carved into or on the face of the rock. A carving in the round, such as figures and animals, is carved on all sides. An assembled or composite carving is comprised of pieces to form one object, such as a flower, in which the petals, buds, and leaves are carved separately, then assembled to make the complete flower. As a beginner, you may want to make several relief carvings or a simple leaf pattern in the round before trying a composite carving.

Many hobbyists make their own tools of soft iron in a variety of shapes and sizes, such as round balls, pointed cones, drilling tubes, or small metal cutoff discs. Iron tools are used with silicon carbide abrasives and water or a light oil. Most small tools can be used on a fixed shaft spindle or on a flex shaft. A fixed shaft spindle leaves both hands free to handle the carving, which can be worked at any angle. Diamond tools such as files and the fine diamond wire saw blades used in a jeweler's saw or coping saw require a light oil or aerosol spray lubricant.

Hobbyists who carve only small objects often prefer to work with a flex shaft after completing the sawing to remove the excess material. When working with larger objects, you could use silicon carbide for all the roughing out and shaping and then smaller diamond tools for the fine details.

Carving in the Round

Before starting a carving in the round, make a clay model so that you can make corrections as you design the piece, using the model as a guide. Another popular method is to draw the design on paper, make all the corrections, then ink the pattern to protect it from smearing. Transfer the pattern to the rough gem material and use the sketch as a guide. Remove as much of the excess rock as possible on the trim saw and then grind on the silicon carbide grinding wheel. Always be sure that you do not cut away the guide lines. A grinding wheel 1 inch wide (2.54 cm) and 6 inches in diameter (15.24 cm) will remove quite a bit of the excess and go into some of the curves, so be careful and watch the guide lines.

Wider wheels that are 1½ inches wide (3.81) and 8 inches in diameter

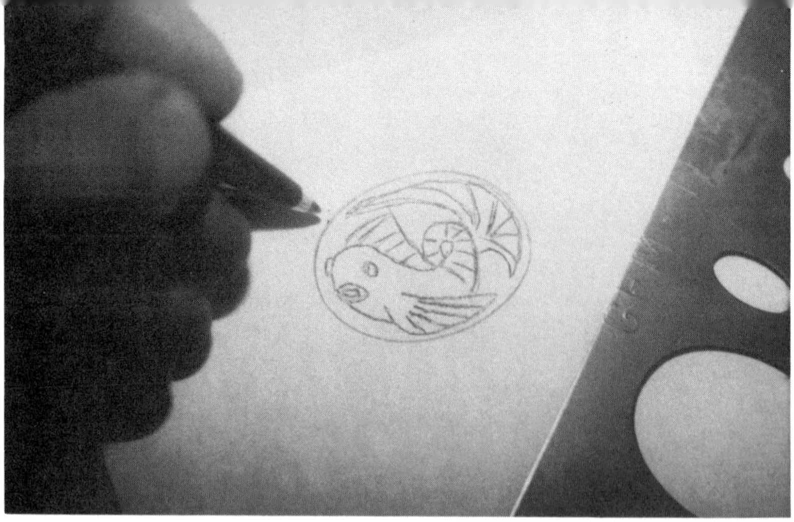

Fig. 9-10 Starting a carving in relief. The design, sketched on paper, is transferred to the slab with carbon paper. However, if the slab has a rough surface, the pattern may have to be sketched directly onto the slab. Photograph by Dale T. Blankenship.

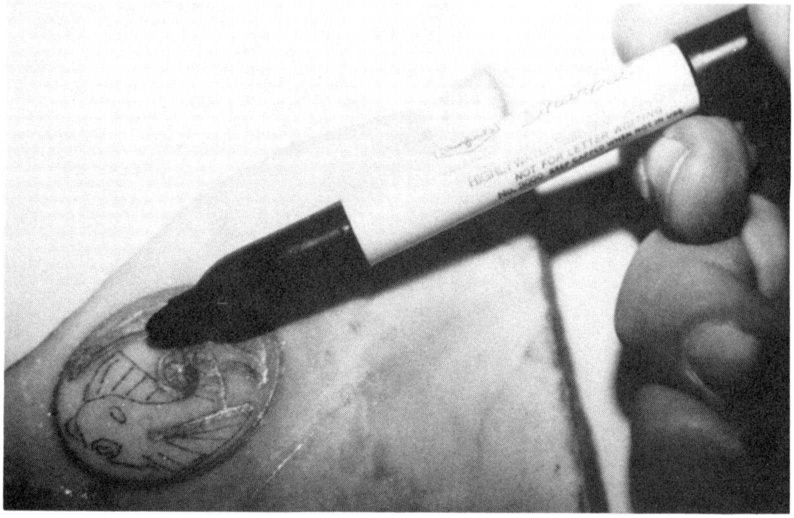

Fig. 9-11 Once the pattern is transferred to the slab, the pattern should be traced with a waterproof marker, then the outside shape marked and cut out. This piece will be a cabochon. Photograph by Dale T. Blankenship.

Fig. 9-12 Shaping the outside edges and sides of the cabochon on a grinding wheel. Photograph by Dale T. Blankenship.

Fig. 9-13 A small design with tight curves can be trimmed on a trim saw, making straight cuts first using a 45° platform so the ends of the cut will be square. Photograph by Dale T. Blankenship.

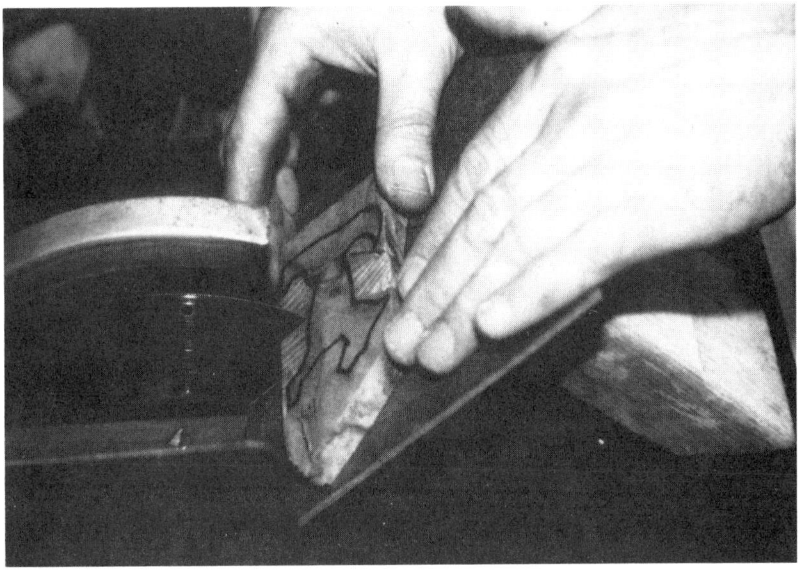

Fig. 9-14 When making straight cuts on the trim saw, the ends of the cuts must be square. Photograph by Dale T. Blankenship.

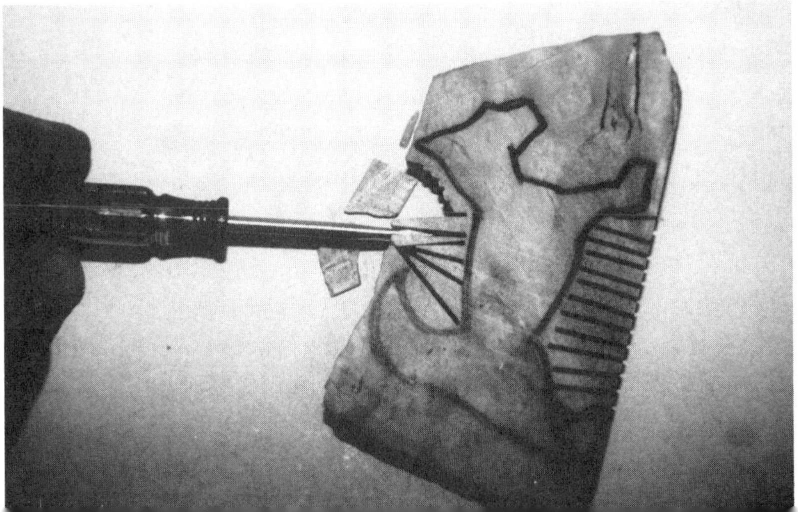

Fig. 9-15 After completing the saw cuts, a strong fine-blade screwdriver can be used to break out the thin layers of stone before grinding, sanding, and polishing. Photograph by Dale T. Blankenship.

(20.32 cm) will not go into curves as well, and do not remove as much rock; and, to get into the curves, you may have to make fine, close parallel cuts into the curve with a saw. If you use the flat bed of the saw, you will undercut the angles. To get a square cut at the end of the cut, place a wooden wedge platform that is slotted to accept the saw blade on the saw table. The wedge should be approximately a 45° angle to make the cut end square. Place the slab material on the wedge and hold it firmly while you make the cut. Then insert a screwdriver between the saw cuts and twist it to break out the excess rock. Then smooth the curves with a smaller wheel and grinding points on a flex shaft. Once you finish the roughing out and shaping, follow the usual procedures of grinding and sanding. Be sure to clean everything between grinds so no coarse grit contaminates the finer grit or polish. Most polishes that are used on cabochons will work well. You may want to semipolish some areas of the carving to accentuate another area.

Carving Bowls and Vases

If you are carving a bowl or ashtray, carve the inside first, leaving the bulk of the gem material on the outside for support. Mark the shape of the hollow and grind it out with silicon carbide balls, which you can make from the cores of old grinding wheels. Or make multiple saw cuts on a trim saw. Use a small-di-

Fig. 9-16 Large shallow bowls are still being made in Idar-Oberstein. The bowl on the right has been ground out, and is ready to be sanded and polished. Photograph by Harold and Erica Van Pelt Photographers.

ameter saw blade for the shallow, shorter cuts. Make the center cut first because this should be the deepest cut. The cuts on either side should be graduated in depth and length. Shorten them gradually to conform to the shape of the inside of the bowl.

When you have made all the parallel cuts, make a few cuts across the center of the original cuts if the center of the bowl is large. These cuts will help you break out the wafers of rock. Break out enough wafers to allow space to insert a small cutoff disc for cutting out the rest of the wafers and smoothing the bowl. If you use a flex shaft with the cutoff disc, be sure to keep the flex shaft dry. A pump spray lubricant works well for most small diamond tools and allows you good control. After cutting out the wafers, grind, sand, and polish the inside of the bowl. (For a large bowl, use silicon carbide for the grinding and sanding since it is less expensive than diamond.)

The outside of the bowl can be finished smooth or you can carve a design in relief. Work cautiously so that you do not risk breaking through the inside of the bowl.

Another method of hollowing out a deeper bowl or a vase is to use core drills. Work out the design on paper and transfer it to the gem material, marking the diameter and depth of the drilling. Depending upon the depth of the interior, you may need more than one drill. Match the size of the core drill and the size and depth of the area to be drilled. If you do not have the exact size, use the next smaller size. Grind and sand away any excess material.

Whether you use a diamond core drill or metal tubing with silicon carbide, you must securely fasten the rough material between wooden blocks and to the base of the drill press. Make a reservoir for the water and abrasive from modeling clay around the area to be drilled. It should be large enough to hold a good supply of grit and water and replenish it as necessary. If you use a diamond drill, use the proper diamond lubricant.

Carefully bring the drill into contact with the rock, then raise and lower it several times until you establish the groove pattern of the cut. Use a guide when getting a large drill tube started. The guide can be a 3⁄8 inch (9.525 mm) to 1⁄2 inch thick (12.7 mm) wooden circle attached to the slab or rock with a dab of dop wax. The guide will help you to establish the cut correctly. Once you have established the cut, remove the guide, especially if you must make a deep cut. Start with light pressure on the drill, then increase the pressure gradually until the cut is finished. Never force a drill beyond its normal motor speed.

Never drill more than a few minutes at a time without raising the bit brief-

Fig. 9-17 In Idar-Oberstein, the cores of the old grinding wheels are smoothed and rounded up, then used to grind the insides of deeper bowls. Photograph by Harold and Erica Van Pelt Photographers.

Fig. 9-18 An Idar-Oberstein worker is sanding the inside of a deep bowl. The inside will be sanded and polished before finishing the outside of the bowl. Photograph by Harold and Erica Van Pelt Photographers.

ly to let new abrasive and water flow under the drill tubing. Continue to raise and lower the drill, using medium pressure, until you complete the drilling. If you are drilling a vase, use a slightly smaller drill than the one used to make the first cut.

If you use a fairly large core drill, the core will remain firmly attached to the bottom of the object. To remove the core, use a smaller drill and drill a series of small holes, one overlapping the other. Remove enough of the small core until you have an area large enough to insert a small diameter cutoff saw blade to cut out the rest of the core. After making several cuts with the saw blade, you may be able to use a larger diameter blade to speed the cutting. When the core is removed, the area can be ground out, sanded, and polished.

Fig. 9-19 A worker in Idar-Oberstein is finishing the outside of the bowl. Photograph by Harold and Erica Van Pelt Photographers.

Fig. 9-20 A gem lathe is ideal for carving symmetrical figures such as chessmen, small vases, bowls, or doorknobs. Courtesy, Gryphon Corporation.

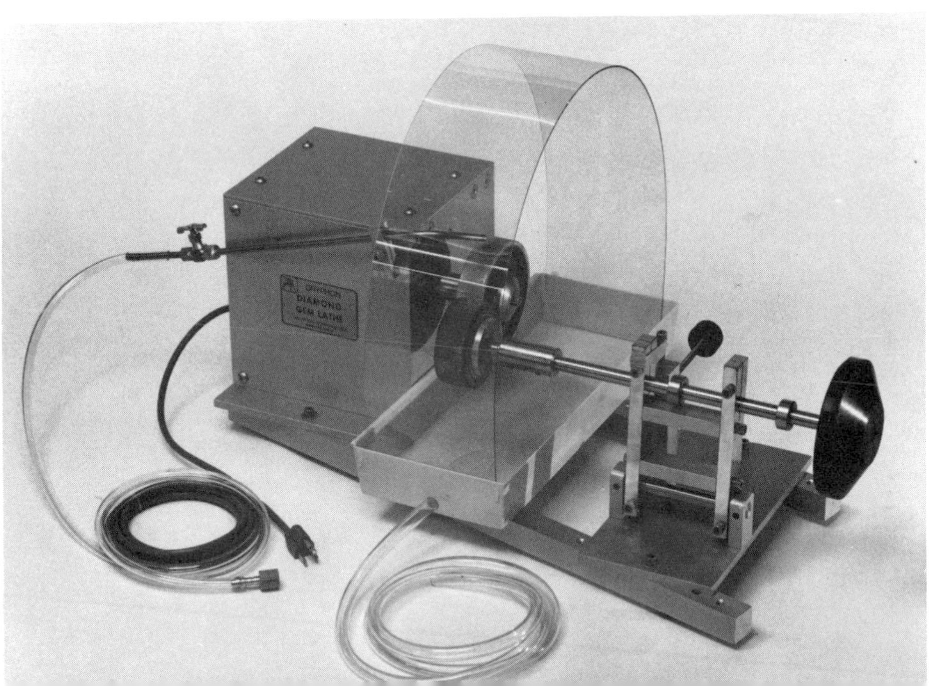

A third method is to use a silicon carbide abrasive ball. If the arbor size of the grinding wheel ball is too large, you may have to buy a larger wheel bushing to fit the stationary spindle.

Studio Visit: Carving a Composite

Olive M. Colhour, an intarsia artist, is also an expert carver. Her favorite subjects are flowers from her garden, as well as figures and animals. When Olive started carving, few tools or lapidary machines were available, so her husband, a skilled machinist, built the tools she needed. She had to learn by trial and error since few books were available. Olive exhibited her first carving and won a trophy, which encouraged her to continue carving. She attends gem and mineral shows in her search for new material and often trades a small carving with a dealer or hobbyist who has a supply of unusual stones.

Her composite carving entitled *Sunshine and Showers* (see color Fig. 27)is a perfect example of Olive's artistry in carving. The delicate roses are a

Fig. 9-21 Olive ground each rose petal separately, then assembled and cemented them into position using the real roses as a pattern. Courtesy, Olive M. Colhour and the Lapidary Journal, Inc.

Fig. 9-22 Olive used tiny cabochons of rock crystal quartz to simulate raindrops on the roses and leaves. Courtesy, Olive M. Colhour and the Lapidary Journal, Inc.

Fig. 9-23 Olive grinds and shapes the jade leaves on a grinding wheel. Courtesy, Olive M. Colhour and the Lapidary Journal, Inc.

Fig. 9-24 Olive uses a micrometer to measure the stems and petals of her flowers so that she can duplicate them exactly. Courtesy, Olive M. Colhour and the Lapidary Journal, Inc.

light pink coral, the leaves are green jade with brown jasper stems, and the raindrops are clear crystalline quartz (rock crystal). The group has three buds in different stages of blossoming, a half-opened rose, and fully opened roses mounted on a base of black granite. It took Olive two and a half months, working five to fourteen hours a day, to complete the project. She used roses from her garden as her model, preserving each petal for complete accuracy.

Olive reproduced each petal, bud, and leaf on her grinding wheels, then assembled the roses and buds using her garden roses as a guide. When she needed some silver or gold accents, she did her own soldering. The finished piece measures 9 inches by 15 inches (22.86 by 38.10 cm). Olive uses micrometers to measure each piece for a perfect fit.

For a pansy arrangement, Olive used two shades of jade for the stems and leaves; the lighter shade was from Alaska and the darker shade was from the Frazier River in Canada. In the calax, she used apple-green jade from Wyoming. Matching the colors for the petals against the real pansies from her garden was difficult. She used different types of agate from Brazil and Mexico, red moss agate fringed with pink and blue agate from Oregon, a lavender agate from Oregon, lapis lazuli from Chili, amethyst from Brazil, and howlite from California. For the bright yellow stamens, she cut a ½ inch thick (12.7 mm) band of yellow from the center of a piece of Australian ribbon jasper. The pansy petals had to be ground extremely thin and beveled where they overlapped.

When Olive starts to assemble the flowers, she makes special molds to hold the blossoms and the centers while the cement dries. For the different pieces of the stems and leaves, she uses Styrofoam blocks. The molds allow her to reposition the flowers before she decides on the final arrangement.

Olive also carves coral branches in the round. A friend sent her a coral branch from Okinawa that she thought looked like a happy figure of a person. She entitled her carving *Happy Fellow*. The carving is about 7 inches (17.78 cm) tall. The hands and foot are branch extensions from the main coral trunk, which was 1½ inches (3.81 cm) in diameter; the base for the carving is 2¾

Fig. 9-25 Olive is soldering the stems together. To add strength to the stems, she often reinforces them with gold or sterling silver wires. Courtesy, Olive M. Colhour and the Lapidary Journal, Inc.

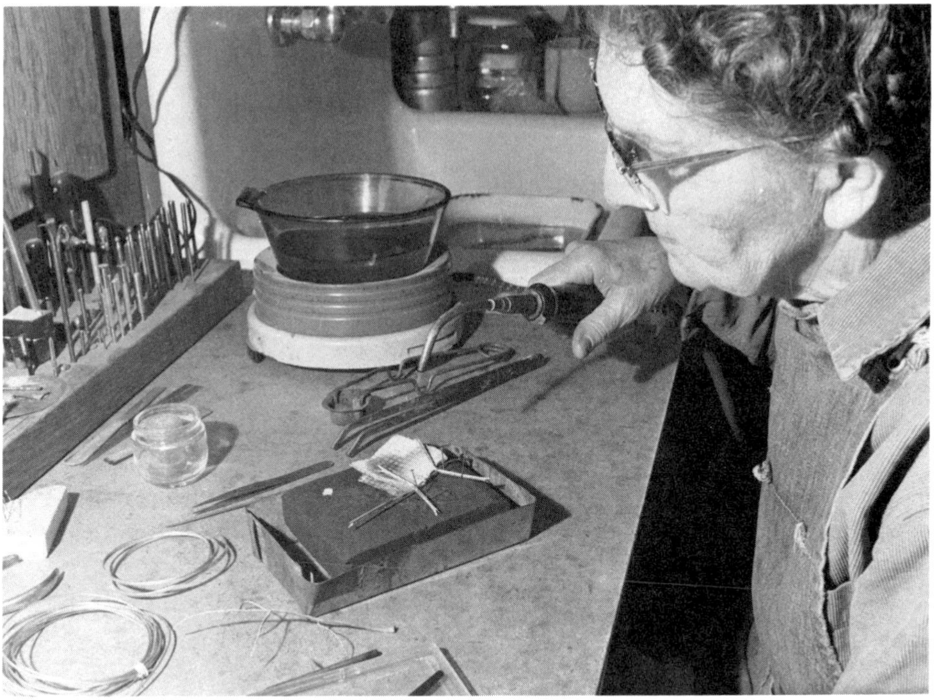

Fig. 9-26 Olive assembles the jade leaves and branch structures. Note the natural leaves on her bench and in the jar of water along side. If the natural leaves wilt, she replaces them with fresh ones. Courtesy, Olive M. Colhour and the Lapidary Journal, Inc.

inches square (6.985 cm). The top square, turned 45° to the main base, is translucent chrysoprase. The leaves on the sides of the base are also chrysoprase, and the flowers are orange jasper. The boxlike base was made as a doublet, with the color layer cemented to the back of the basic gem material and the design carved through to expose colors. The carving was done with a flex shaft and diamond points (see Fig. 9-27) and took Olive about forty hours to complete.

Olive's *Night Raiders*, is a combination carving in the round and a composite. Each unit of the finished object was carved individually. Olive completed the mice and placed them on the composite carving (see Fig. 9-29). The mice are silver-sheen obsidian with sterling silver feet and tails, and the cheese squares are honey onyx. Olive tapered and knurled the tails before cementing them to the bodies, and the feet were made like gloves and cemented to the obsidian legs. The black jade eyes are cemented in place. The dish, 4½ inches

Fig. 9-27 Happy Fellow, a carving in the round from a coral branch, 7 inches high (17.78 cm). It is also a composite, since the base was carved separately and then attached to the coral figure. Courtesy, Olive M. Colhour and the Lapidary Journal, Inc.

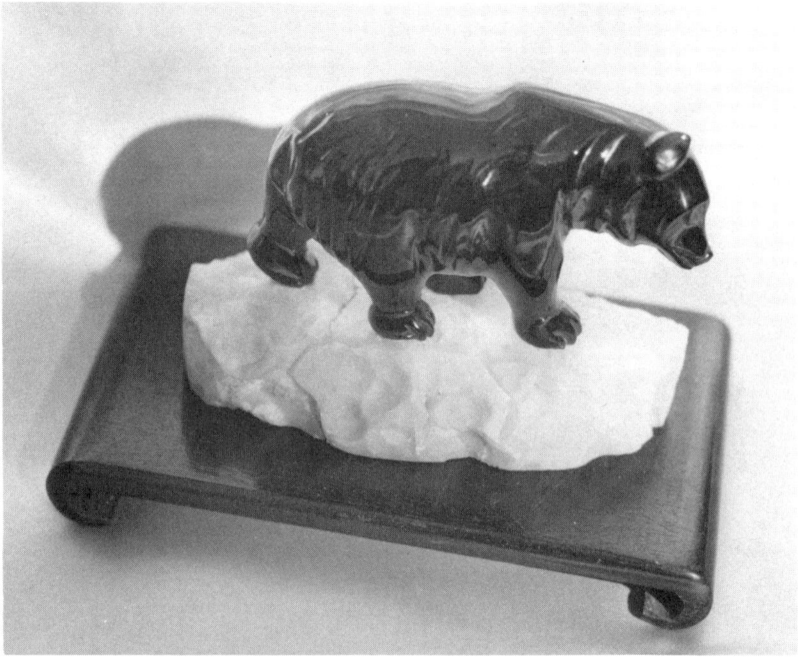

Fig. 9-28 The bear is both a carving in the round and a composite carving because the white-snow base is a separately carved piece and the bear is cemented to it. Courtesy, Olive M. Colhour.

Fig. 9-29 The Night Raiders, carved from silver-sheen obsidian, have sterling silver feet and tails. Courtesy, Olive M. Colhour and the Lapidary Journal, Inc.

square (11.43 cm), is clear agate with tortoise shell reflections interspersed with areas of chrysoprase.

Studio Visit: Carving in the Round

Dale T. Blankenship specializes in carving nephrite jade. When Dale started *Chameleon and the Moth* (Fig. 9-30), he had already done the preliminary work of removing the outer excess of the jade and had done the general shaping. He used no diamond tools until he was almost finished. *Chameleon and the Moth* was an award winner. One of Dale's most recent carvings is a pair of obsidian bats (see color Fig. 17).

Dale uses a carving spindle mounted on the end of his bench. He uses grinding wheels 8 inches (20.32 cm) in diameter by 1½ inches (3.81 cm) thick. This size wheel is not adaptable for sharp inside curves, but it is excellent for removing excess material from outside curves. For deep inside curves, Dale makes straight parallel cuts on a trim saw by using a 45° platform wedge to be sure the ends of the cuts are square. He holds the slab firmly on the wedge, stopping the cut just short of his guide lines (see Fig. 9-14).

Dale smooths the inside curves on the carving spindle with silicon car-

Fig. 9-30 The Chameleon and the Moth by Dale Blankenship was carved from spinach-green nephrite.

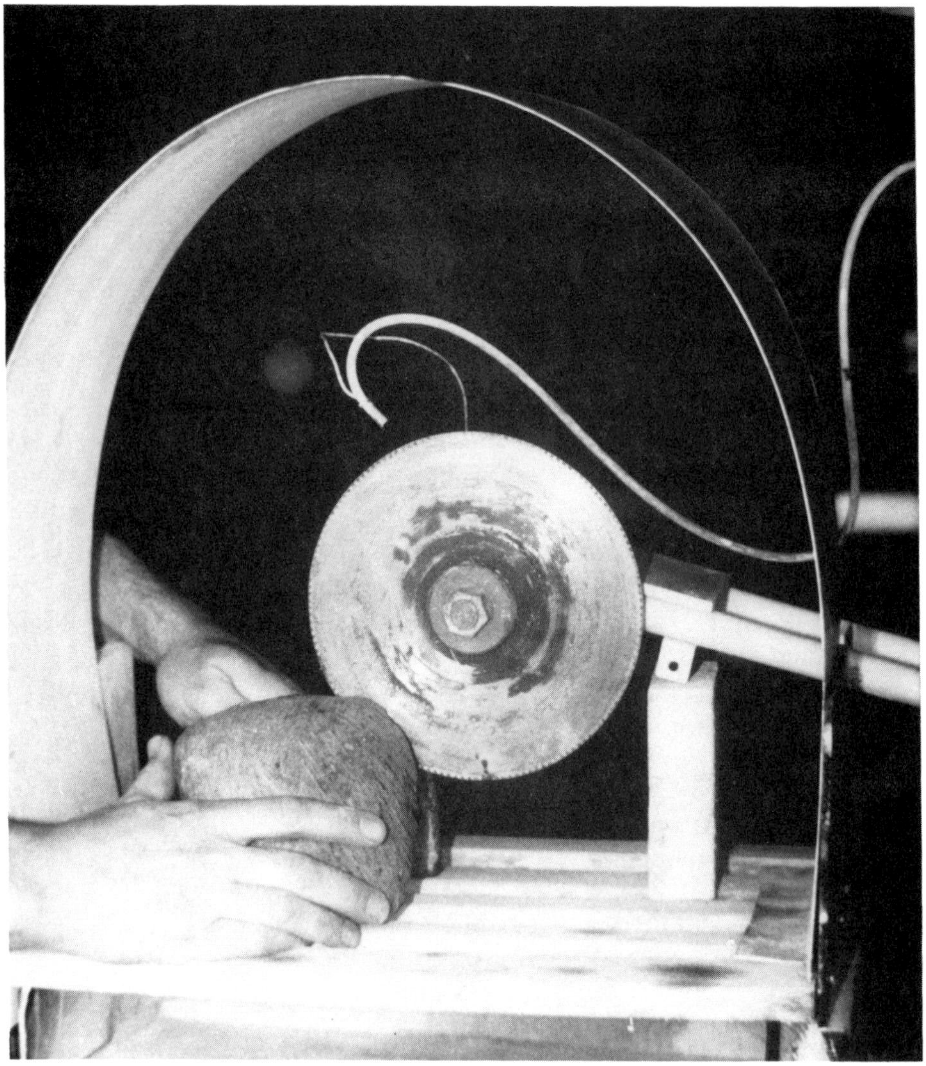

Fig. 9-31 A saw blade or a grinding wheel can be used in this saw. It is similar to some used by Oriental carvers. Photograph by Dale T. Blankenship.

Fig. 9-32 Dale uses a flex shaft with small diamond tools for working in small, fine-detailed areas. Courtesy, Foredom Electric Company.

Fig. 9-33 The Princess and the Frog carved from spinach-green nephrite jade, by Dale Blankenship. The wooden stand has been cut out to accept the carving but is not permanently attached.

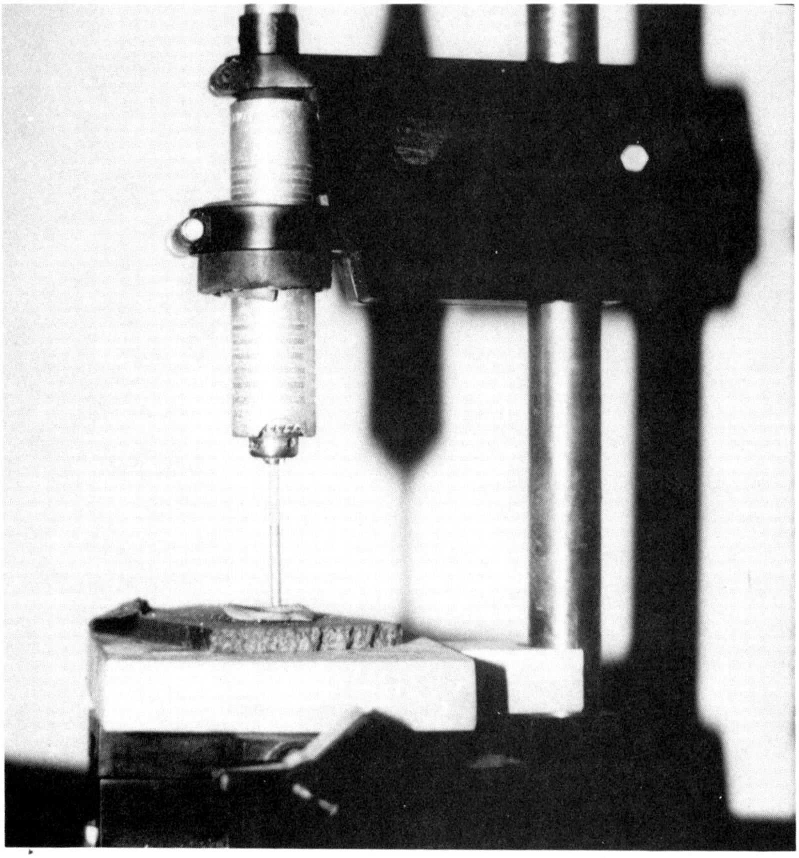

Fig. 9-34 If Dale needs to drill a small hole in a piece of gem material, he clamps his flex-shaft handpiece into a drill stand so that he can drill the holes without breaking the drill bit. Note the clay well formed around the area to be drilled to hold the slurry. Photograph by Dale T. Blankenship.

Fig. 9-35 Hard felt points and wheels can be used with a flex shaft to polish small difficult areas. Courtesy, Foredom Electric Company.

bide points or a small ball. Sometimes he uses a flex shaft with small silicon carbide tools, rubber-bonded points, or diamond points and discs for sanding. The carving spindle can accommodate any small cutoff blades or silicon carbide grinding points made from old wheels, as well as diamond points or polishing buffs.

To make fine, delicate lines and cuts, Dale works with diamond points, using either his carving spindle or flex shaft. When he sands small areas, he uses rubber-bonded abrasives, which are available in several sizes and shapes of cones or wheels and in coarse, medium, and fine grit sizes. He also uses small hard felt flat wheels, knife-edge wheels, or points, as well as small cotton flannel buffs and diamond accessories for polishing.

Dale's drill press requires that the rough material be securely attached to the drill base before drilling. When Dale uses a tube drill and silicon carbide abrasives, he forms a well with modeling clay to hold the watery abrasive mixture. To drill fine holes, Dale mounts his flex shaft in his drill base and uses diamond drills with a pump spray lubricant.

Studio Visit: Carving a Wide Variety of Material

Maury and Opal Maline are experienced hobbyists who learned carving on their own and sometimes work together on a single carving. Maury made their

Fig. 9-36 Maury Maline carved this Oriental-style hydra on a botryoidal piece of gem chrysocolla. He left part of the gem chrysocolla in its natural shape as background for the carving. Photograph by Maury Maline.

carving arbor and assembled the various tools. He built the arbor to accommodate small tools used with a silicon carbide slurry, as well as diamond tools, such as old dental tools, drills, and diamond-charged burrs and points. Maury and Opal also acquired a flex shaft.

Maury and Opal do their preliminary shaping on an 8 inch by 1½ inch (20.32 by 3.81 cm) wheel. They use the carving arbor with a slurry of silicon carbide abrasive for further shaping and to remove material in smaller areas. They accomplish their fine details with the flex shaft and fine diamond points, in addition to other small tools. Maury and Opal have assembled several prize-winning exhibits of their small carvings, including a Brazilian rock crystal statuette with the trim and base of rhodochrosite from Argentina (see color Fig.

15), the head of a Madonna carved in opal with a fiery play of color, and the head of a native girl carved in golden-sheen obsidian, all carved by Opal. Maury included the head of a hippo carved in black jade with a mouth lined with Argentinian rhodochrosite and the teeth carved from California howlite. Other carvings in the exhibit were a variscite frog and jumping fish, a stylized Chinese chow dog design, and a bullfrog carved in California black jade, which took Maury 500 hours to complete and a tigereye snail (see color Fig. 18). One of his more recent carvings is an oriental-style hydra (water dragon) on lotus leaves (Fig. 9-36), carved from a fine piece of translucent chrysoprase.

PART FOUR

FACETED STONES

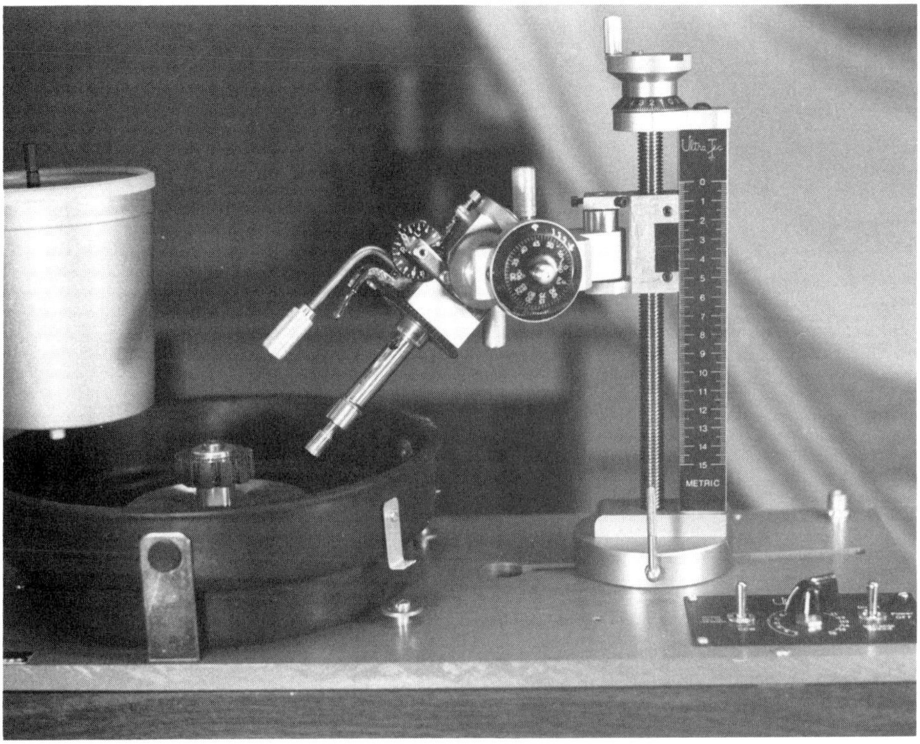

10

FACETING GEMSTONES

Faceting became evident in Europe about 1290, when a guild of gem cutters and polishers was established in France. Most of the guild's efforts were directed to the cutting and polishing of diamonds rather than colored stones, with the exception of garnets, which were given just a rose cut. English lapidaries were cutting colored gemstones as early as 1775. Idar-Oberstein, Germany (now West Germany), had been a colored-stone center since 1454, but it was not until 1875 that artisans began faceting. In the late nineteenth century, gemstone centers began to emerge throughout Europe.

The earliest machine method of faceting, which continued until the early 1960s, was the jam-peg method. This was comprised of a vertical rod and a rectangular block backrest that was slightly curved over the top edge and had symmetrically drilled holes on the backrest or a cone so that the faceter could achieve the proper angle on the stone. A dop stick, tapered on both ends and shaped like an elongated, old-fashioned desk pen, was used to hold the stone. The long end was tapered to a slightly rounded point and inserted in the backrest, which was positioned on a vertical shaft or rod set up next to a horizontal flat lap. The laps were usually hardwood or metal. The angles of the facets were changed by using the different holes in the backrest. The angle of the backrest could also be changed. All cutting was done by eye, since there were no machines for calibrating angles or degrees, and most of the equipment was homemade.

When starting to learn to facet, it is helpful to have an instructor. How-

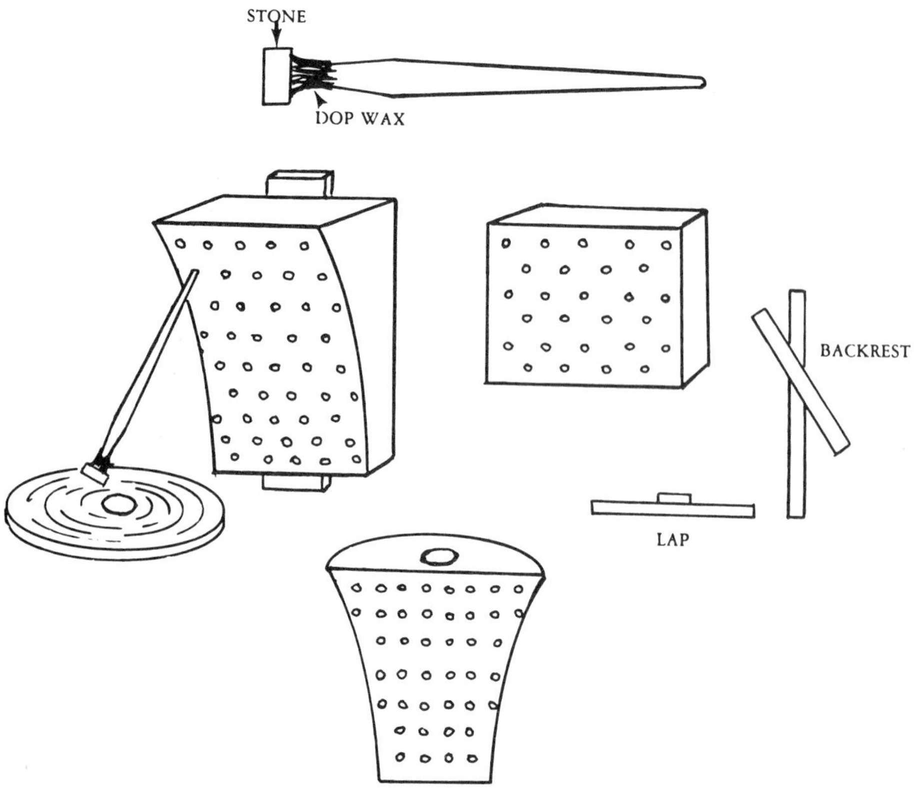

Fig. 10-1 Jam-peg faceting, the first method of faceting. This illustration shows the variations of the backrest used by the early faceters. Illustration by Dara E. Yost.

ever, if an instructor is not available, there are several good books designed to teach the beginner to facet without the aid of an instructor. You can also contact a gem and mineral club; many of them conduct classes or will be able to direct you to an instructor.

CUTTING METHODS

When cutting a stone, you can cut either the crown (top) or the pavilion (bottom) first. But there are several factors to consider before you decide on the faceted shape of the stone, such as size, transparency, color, and brilliance. Colorless or light-colored stones should be cut for brilliance, whereas highly

Fig. 17 The Bats at Rest, by Dale T. Blankenship. The black obsidian bats are 5½ inches (13.97 cm) high and 4 inches (10.16 cm) wide. Photograph by the artist.

Fig. 18 A tigereye snail carved by Maury Maline. Photograph by the artist.

Fig. 19 *Gypsy Rhythm*, a sculptured intarsia, is one of Olive M. Colhour's early pieces. Courtesy, the artist and the Lapidary Journal, Inc.

Fig. 20 *El Picaro* ("The Rascal") produced by Olive M. Colhour from her original watercolor. Courtesy, the artist and the Lapidary Journal, Inc.

Fig. 21 These Are Mine, a recent intarsia made by Olive M. Colhour, is a reproduction of the artist's hands. Courtesy, the artist and the Lapidary Journal, Inc.

Fig. 22 *The Town Clock*, by William E. Grundke. A cobblestone street scene with the clock tower at the end of the street. Courtesy, the artist.

Fig. 23 *The Sleigh Ride*, by William E. Grundke. He uses howlite for most snow scenes because of its pure white color. Courtesy, the artist.

Fig. 24 A modern sugilite carving by Hing Wa Lee, with a symbolic dragon on the front and a phoenix bird on the back. The carving is 2⅞ inches (73.025 mm) high and 1½ inches (38.1 mm) wide; the depth is ⅞ inch (22.225 mm). The stand is ¾ inch (19.05 mm) high. Photograph by Warren Bowen Photography.

Fig. 25 A jadeite carving of a celestial child worshipping the Goddess of Mercy (Kwan Yin) in the East Seas, by Hing Wa Lee. The background designs are bamboo and a phoenix bird. The jadeite is light lavender, with faint tinges of yellow green. The carving is 9 inches (22.86 cm) high, 6 inches (15.24 cm) wide and 5 inches (12.7 cm) deep; the stand is 1½ inches (38.1 mm) high. Photograph by Warren Bowen Photography.

Fig. 26 This rhodonite rose carved by Maury Maline won the Gem Carvers Guild of America trophy with 100 points in 1983. Photograph by Charles Boblenz. Courtesy, the artist.

Fig. 27 Sunshine and Showers, carved by Olive M. Colhour. The roses are a light pink gem coral and the leaves are nephrite jade with gold-wire veining. The raindrops are rock-crystal cabochons. Courtesy, the artist and the Lapidary Journal, Inc.

Fig. 10-2 Earl Manor of San Diego, California, demonstrates faceting at a local gem and mineral show. Photograph by A. D. Daegling, Jr.

colored stones should be cut to bring out the best color. In some instances, this will mean cutting the pavilion part of the stone shallower than normal.

Before you start, examine the rough gemstone carefully to determine the direction of best color and the inclusions. Heavy inclusions can be avoided by cutting through the inclusion and faceting two stones instead of one, or you can move the stone a little to the right or left. Some gem materials are highly color-zoned. If the best spot or section of color can be oriented at the bottom of the pavilion, then, when the stone is viewed face up (through the table of the stone), the entire stone will have good color.

When you begin faceting, get into the habit of keeping a record of exactly what has been done and of the settings that were used on the faceting unit. Then, if you must recut a facet to meet another, or if you are interrupted dur-

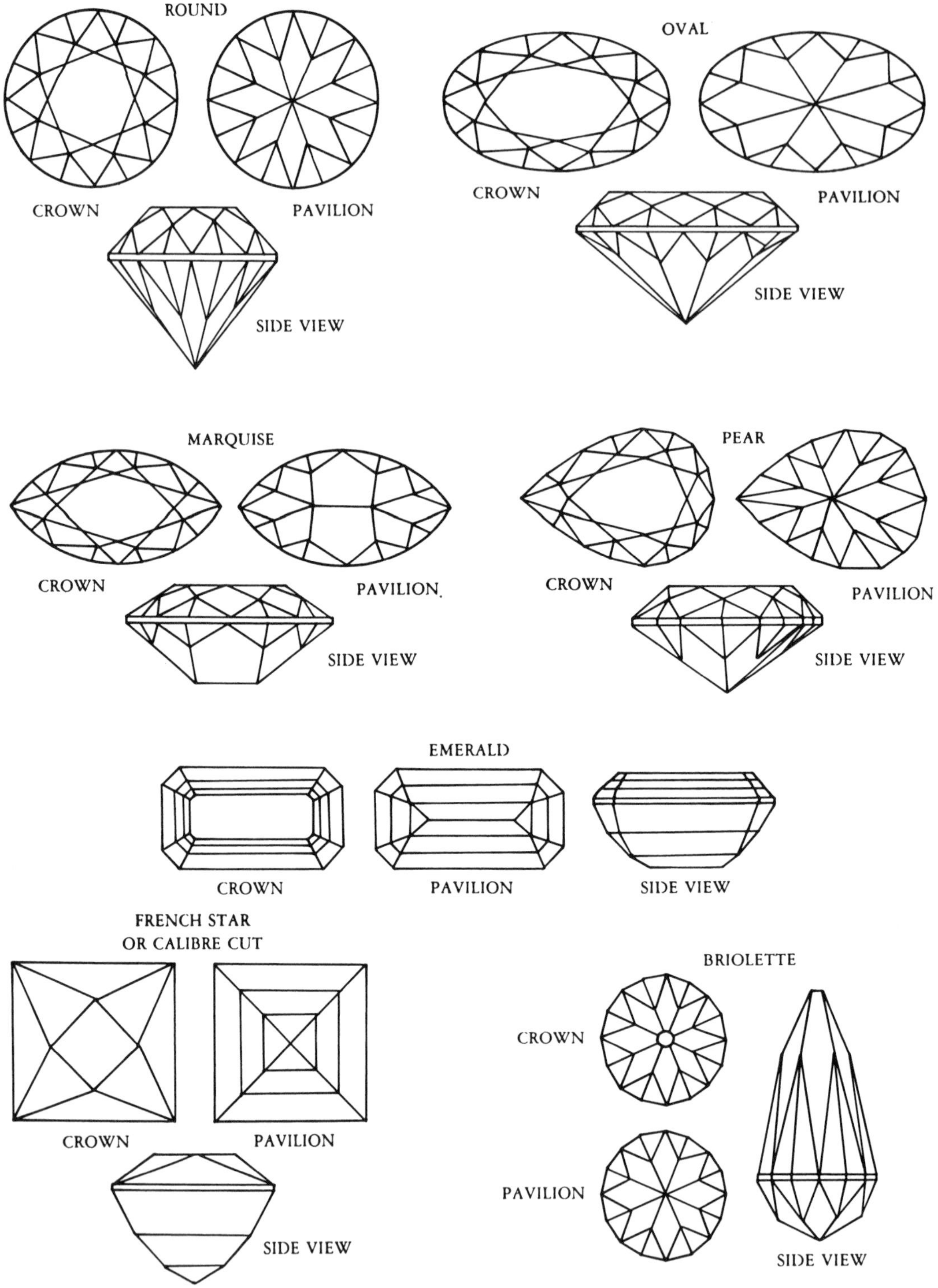

Fig. 10-3 The seven basic faceting designs. Illustration by Gerd E. F. Sittel.

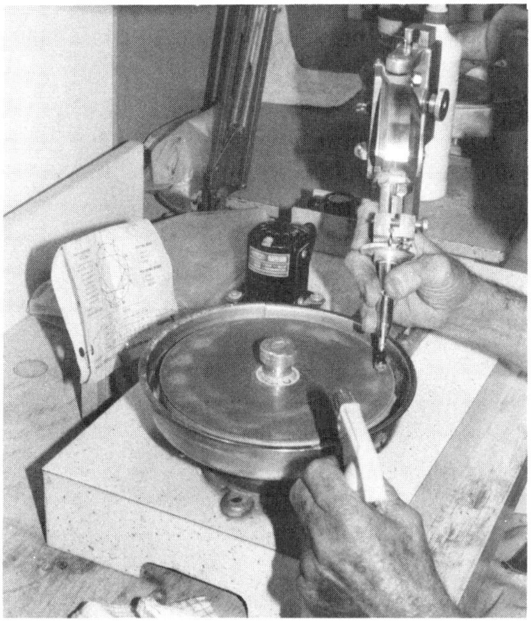

Fig. 10-4 Rough grinding the crown of a stone. Note the diagram propped up in front of the lapidary. The spray bottle contains lubricant for the lap.

Fig. 10-5 A section of the lap pan has been removed so that the faceter can cut the girdle of the stone. This section is also removed to clean the lap pan of the faceting unit.

ing the cutting, you can check at a glance the quadrant positions (degrees), the index, the angles, and the order in which the cutting was accomplished.

As you learn faceting, you will learn how to cut opposite facets. For example, if you cut the main crown facet at 96 on the index gear, you can cut the opposite crown at 48 on the index gear. Some faceters do all the cutting first, then go back and do all the polishing. Others cut and polish each facet separately, as they work around the stone. If you cut the stone first and save all the polishing until last, you will need a record of the settings to refer to when you reset the angles and degrees and the order of grind (the sequence in which the facets are cut) in order to polish the stone. Good light is essential.

The basic faceting designs—oval, marquise, pear, emerald, French star (or calibre cut), and briolette—are shown in Fig. 10-3. New cuts designed by advanced faceting hobbyists are usually based on a round cut, emerald cut, square cut, or rectangular cut, although some faceters cut free-form cut stones to conserve the maximum amount of stone. The various faceting cuts for brilliant-cut and emerald-cut stones are shown in Fig. 10-7.

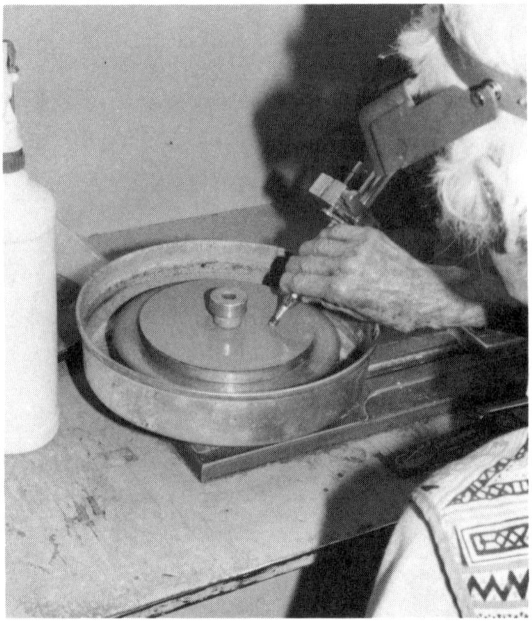

Fig. 10-6 Polishing a stone. Note the position of her hand on the dop stick as she moves the stone across the lap.

The rose cut, which probably originated in India, was often used for garnets and has several variations: a three-facet cut, a six-facet cut, the full rose cut, and a double-rose cut. The double-rose cut is the same as two rose cuts back to back. A single rose cut has a flat, smooth base, and the facets on the top all meet at a center point. It does not have a table facet and usually has a low dome contour when viewed from the side. This cut is now very seldom used.

The ideal cut of a faceted stone should have the following proportions: The table (the large flat spot on the top of the faceted stone) is approximately one-half the diameter of the stone. The crown of the stone (the top section above the girdle line) is one-third of the stone's height. The girdle (the thin line between the crown and the pavilion) usually accounts for 1½% to 2% of the depth of the entire stone. And the pavilion (the lower portion of the stone) is two-thirds of the depth of the finished stone.

If the stone is to be a brilliant, well-cut gemstone, its proportions must be correct. Properly cut stones will reflect the maximum light from inside the

DOPPING THE STONE

Dopping is an important part of the faceting process. If a stone is not properly dopped, it will fall off the dop stick and you will have difficulty matching up the facets. If this happens, the stone will have to be recut to a smaller size. Always use new *faceting wax rather than the green dopping wax used for cabochons. Clean the stone first in denatured alcohol to remove any grease or oil. Then coat the stone with colorless liquid shellac before dopping.*

Handle the stone with tweezers, and use a dop stick that is about two-thirds the size of the stone. Do not allow the dop wax to burn or sizzle as that will weaken the holding power of the wax. If the wax gets directly into the flame and discolors, it will not hold well. Overheated wax will turn brittle and will not hold the stone properly.

You will need a transfer plate, or faceplate dop, which is a dop stick with a round disc of metal mounted at a right angle to the shank. When you cut the crown of the stone before the pavilion, you must dop the preform straight and true. Insert the faceplate into the left side of the transfer block. After dopping the pavilion part of the preform and the dop wax is still warm, insert the dopped preform into the right side of the transfer block. Rewarm both dop sticks mounted by holding the transfer block and the dop sticks over the alcohol lamp. Then press the dop sticks together to straighten the preform in the dop so it will be square and the crown will be cut straight and true.

If the piece is fairly small, you may not wish to preform it first. If you do not preform the stone, select the area for the table and grind it perfectly flat on your lap, then dop the stone using the same method as for a preform stone.

You will also need a 45° dop with a square metal block mounted on the end. The metal block is drilled at an angle of 45°. When the dop arm of the faceting machine is set at the same angle, the block allows the dopped stone to be held at a 90° angle to ensure that the table of the stone can be cut absolutely true and flat.

Keep the wax warm while you dop the stone by holding the center of the dop stick over a low flame of the alcohol lamp or under an infrared heat lamp. If the dop stick becomes too hot to handle, take a section of a wooden broom handle that is a convenient length to work with and drill a ¼ inch (6.35 mm) hole in the center and insert the end of the dop stick.

If the gemstone is heat-sensitive, work under a heat lamp or use the cold-dopping method. For cold dopping, some hobbyists use a liquid cement or quick-set epoxies. The stone must then be soaked in a cement thinner or remover to loosen it from the dop stick. Others use cyanocrylates since dopped stones can be soaked loose in acetone, nail-polish remover containing acetone (but not the oily *polish remover), or nitro methane.*

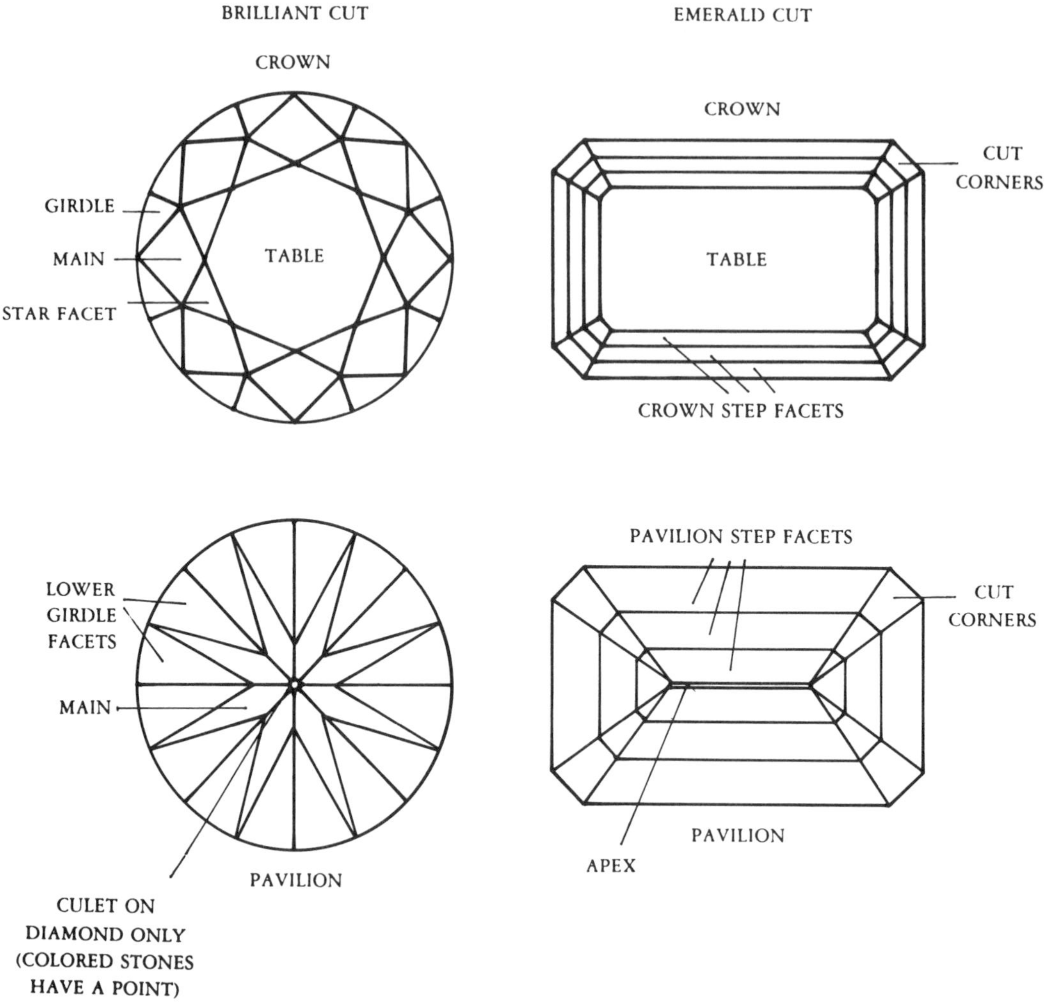

Fig. 10-7 Faceting diagram for a round brilliant cut and an emerald cut. The facets on a square or rectangular cut are the same as the emerald cut. Illustration by Gerd E. F. Sittel.

stone. Total reflection from inside the stone is the cause of brilliance. Most faceting instruction books recommend that the pavilion of a round brilliant gemstone be cut at angles from 39° to 43°, depending upon the material, in order to obtain the maximum brilliance from the pavilion. The crown is usually cut with facets from 30° to 40° or from 40° to 50°, depending on the refractive index, and in proportion to the angles used for the pavilion. Most faceting instruction manuals include charts showing recommended angles for the

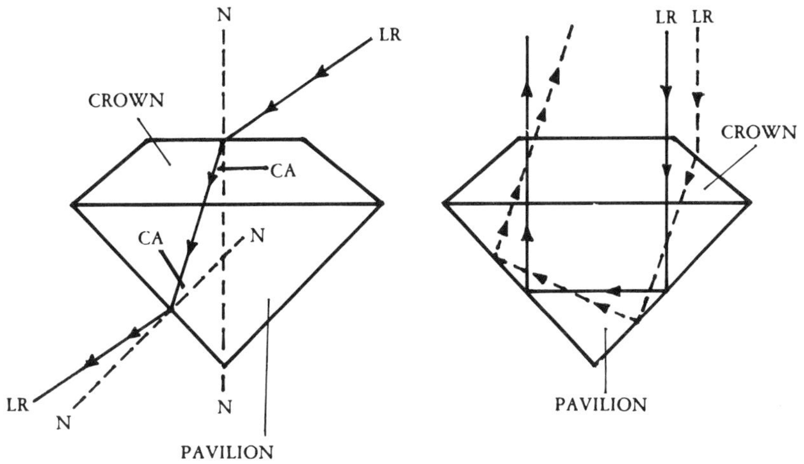

Fig. 10-8 Refracted and reflected light: the diagram on the left shows refracted light from the back of the stone; the diagram on the right shows total reflection. Illustration by Gerd E. F. Sittel.

N = THE NORMAL
(AN IMAGINARY LINE)

LR = THE SINGLE
LIGHT RAY

CA = CRITICAL ANGLE
(OCCURS ONLY
INSIDE THE STONE)

crown and pavilion, as well as the critical angles and the recommended polishing laps and polishes.

There are several terms concerning light reaction that should be understood. When light strikes the surface of a stone, but does not enter the stone, the light is reflected away at the same angle at which it strikes the surface of the stone, and is called *reflected light*. When light strikes the surface of a gemstone at any angle other than the normal angle (an imaginary line perpendicular to the surface of the stone that continues straight through the stone) and enters the gemstone, it will be bent slightly toward the normal. The bending of light within the gemstone is called *refraction*. Refraction occurs only *within* the gemstone. Upon leaving the gemstone, the light continues at the same angle it entered the stone.

The angle formed inside the gemstone that is between the bent ray and the normal becomes the *critical angle*. Any light inside the stone that strikes within the critical angle will "leak out" of the pavilion of the stone. A stone that is cut too shallow or too deep will not return a maximum amount of light back through the crown and will appear dull.

When the stone is cut to the proper angles, it will reflect the light internally and return it through the crown to the eye of the observer. This is considered *total reflection* and is what most hobbyists try to achieve. Remember, critical angle is not the angle at which the pavilion facets are cut. (See the Appendix for a chart of refractive indexes and their critical angles.)

Once you become proficient in faceting, you can experiment with unusual cuts or design your own faceting cuts and submit them to one of the lapidary magazines.

Studio Visit: Faceting Novelties

Jerry Muchna is an outstanding faceter who specializes in novelties. Jerry uses only colorless Brazilian quartz and occasionally rutilated quartz. His subjects include a variety of still-lifes, animated figures, mechanical figures, and animal forms. Jerry works in Brazilian quartz because he can obtain pieces that are large enough and comparatively free of inclusions and flaws.

FACETING LARGE GEMSTONES

Axel B. Pederson is an accomplished faceter who often works with large gemstones. Axel cuts tiny facets and often makes them elongated, as on a briolette. The gemstones are similar to faceted balls, except that they are a little wider in diameter than they are high. The gemstone on the left was approximately ¾ inch (19.05 mm) in diameter at the widest part and just a fraction shorter. The stone in the center is approximately 1 inch (25.4 mm) high and almost the same in diameter.

Fig. 10-9 Three gemstones cut by Axel B. Pedersen. The stone on the left, a high-lead glass, is slightly smaller than the other two and has a table. The gemstone in the center is smoky quartz and the one on the right is also high-lead glass.

Jerry uses an M.D.R. faceting unit. He has also built and adapted his own machine parts for cutting concave facets, using sewing machine parts, some computer parts, and vibrator parts. Jerry spends days planning out his faceting projects and begins by shaping and molding clay models of his subject.

Jerry never writes down the degrees or indexing, since he finds holding the degrees more challenging. He also finds it is easier to change laps than to change degrees and indexing. He cuts, rough grinds, fine grinds, and polishes each facet before going to the next one, so he never has to reset the degrees or indexing before polishing the facets.

One of Jerry's early faceted novelties is *Crystal City*, which is comprised of 21 items with 5,528 facets and weighs 5,566 carats. Jerry does his preforming on a well-dressed, smooth 220 grit grinding wheel, then takes the piece directly to his faceting unit. He sometimes straightens out or trues all flat areas on a 230 grit diamond lap, then changes to the 400 grit diamond lap, and, if necessary, goes to the 1,200 grit diamond lap, completing the polishing with cerium oxide on a vinyl lap. Jerry has been faceting various pieces for his *Crystal City* for the last ten years.

When Jerry faceted a seal balancing a rutilated quartz ball, he had to improvise his own equipment for cutting and polishing the concave facets. This was a difficult project because the concave facets had to form the proper curves. The seal has six parts, with a total of 884 facets on the seal and 288 facets to form the ball.

One of Jerry's most difficult projects was a rose with three sets of four petals, all completely faceted, and a small bud enclosed in the center. The rose is cemented onto a flat square of quartz, 1/4 inch (6.35 mm) thick and 1 inch (25.4 mm) square, and mounted on a half sphere of quartz. He cut the first set of petals from a slice of quartz crystal 1/2 inch (12.7 mm) thick. The finished petals were 3/8 inch (9.525 mm) thick, 1 3/8 inches (34.925 mm) high, and 1 1/2 inches (38.1 mm) wide at the top, tapering to 1 inch (25.4 mm) at the bottom.

Jerry cut the outer edges of the petals with concave facets so that they would display a more graceful curve than could be produced by the usual flat facets. The second set of rose petals measured 5/16 inch (7.9375 mm) thick and were tapered from 1 inch (25.4 mm) at the top to 1/4 inch (6.35 mm) at the bottom, with concave facets on the outer edges. Jerry cut the bottoms at an angle for more ease in mounting. He cut the third set of leaves straight, without concave facets. They measured 1 inch (25.4 mm) high and 3/8 inch (9.525 mm) to 1/4 inch (6.35 mm) in width.

Jerry fitted the petals around the center bud, which he faceted like a tear-

Fig. 10-10 The Spirit of St. Louis is one of Jerry Muchna's recent additions to his "Great Moments in America" series. It is faceted from Brazilian quartz. Photograph by Bob Jones.

drop. The slant was critical. The degree of slant would determine the final angle at which the petals would rest. A 50° angle would produce an open flower, while a 75° slant would result in a closed flower. Jerry knew it would be difficult to attach all of the petals with epoxy cement in the small area produced by the 75° angle, so he chose the 50° angle. The bottom of the bud was no problem for Jerry—he simply made it a half sphere. The finished sphere contained 147 facets and the rose more than 1,000 facets.

A faceted daisy which he cut, required cutting dual-axial off-center facets on the surface of the petals. Jerry had to gently heat the dopped stone and rotate it by hand as he finished each facet. The finished daisy required 488 facets, had a total carat weight of 163 carats, and took 86 hours to complete.

Jerry has turned some of his talents to the recording of American historical events in a collection of quartz miniatures entitled "Great Moments in America." The collection includes *The Statue of Liberty, The Spirit of Seventy-six,* and *Iwo Jima*.

Jerry's most complex and demanding project was the raising of the American flag on Iwo Jima, which has 6,511 facets and took 540 hours to complete. Each figure has more than 1,000 facets and the total weight of the faceted figures is 1,721 carats. Jerry had difficulty cementing the figures together so that they looked natural. First he had to glue the arms and legs to the body with white glue. He had so much difficulty positioning the arms and legs to the body that he found it necessary to use his wife as a model before he could make them look natural. Then he had to clean off the white glue, repolish, and recement them with epoxy. The base, representing Mt. Suribachi, was fired clay stained to simulate the volcanic rock.

Jerry's *Spirit of St. Louis* (see color Fig. 16) has a total weight of 880 carats. The airplane, covered with 695 facets, has 30 separate pieces of quartz, each cut to size and faceted. The one-piece engine nacelle was the most difficult part of the whole project. The other pieces are the fuselage, the two wings, two ailerons, seven struts, the wheels, the propeller (made in three pieces), and the tail assembly (made in five pieces). Jerry's pieces always have a superb polish. They are clean, with sharp-edged facets and are scratch-free and smooth. Even though most of his novelties are unusual shapes and cannot always be cut to the proportions that result in maximum brilliance, he always obtains good dispersion and brilliance.

11

FACETING EQUIPMENT

Faceting is the art of cutting and polishing a transparent gemstone by placing small, flat polished faces, or facets, over the top and bottom surfaces of the stone in a symmetrical pattern.

The earliest hobbyists in the United States, in the late 1930s and early 1940s, found it difficult to obtain information on faceting. Their only sources were a few Old World journeymen who had emigrated to the United States and found jobs in the large, well-established jewelry houses. But few of the artisan-craftsmen would divulge their cutting secrets, since it was their only way to earn a living.

In the late 1940s and early 1950s, some faceters who were machinists and tool planners by trade began to improvise mechanical faceting units that would do the same work with more mathematical and symmetrical accuracy. Soon mechanical faceting units began to enter the market.

FACETING UNITS AND MASTER LAPS

Faceting units have become more elaborate in recent years with the addition of electronic gauges and stops. Many faceting units can be set on a flat-top desk or table. The desk or table must be solid to prevent vibration, which can cause excessive wear on the faceting machine.

The faceting unit is comprised of a faceting head and a master lap. The faceting head incorporates several parts: the mast or stand rod that can be either a round, smooth rod or a rack-and-pinion assembly. It is mounted on a

Fig. 11-1 One of many faceting units made for the hobbyist. Courtesy, Norman T. Jarvi Company.

metal base that is slotted so that the stand rod can be moved back and forth to allow for accurate positioning of the dopped gemstone over the master lap assembly. The metal base is mounted to a desk, table or a sturdy base of its own so that it can be portable. On newer machines, the rack-and-pinion stand rod provides a more accurate method of adjusting the height of the dop arm. A sleeve assembly is placed on the mast or stand rod, which has a wing nut or knurled screw for tightening or loosening the sleeve adjustment. The dop arm is mounted on the sleeve and extends away from the mast or stand rod. The dop arm has a chuck or fitting on the left that holds the dop stick tightly in place.

A notched index gear, and a gear trigger which holds the index gear in the selected position, is mounted on the right end of the dop arm. A pointer is located toward the center of the dop arm and indicates the position that has been set on the quadrant. The quadrant is similar to a protractor and is used to set the angle of elevation. It is mounted on the sleeve or on another part of the head assembly, depending on the type of faceting head. The dop arm extends from the sleeve over the master lap assembly.

The lap assembly is mounted on the same base that the faceting head is mounted on and is set at the end of the metal base of the facet head on the lefthand side of the stand rod. The master lap and its drip pan are mounted on an arbor that has a ½ inch (12.7 mm) shaft that runs horizontally and extends far enough above the master lap to hold any other lap that is placed on the master lap. The nut on the end of the shaft is usually knurled so that it can be easily tightened or loosened to change any lap that may be needed.

On the dop arm is a second small pointer or benchmark located close enough to the index gear to indicate what index gear is being used. Most faceting heads come with one index gear, either a 96 index or a 64 index gear, and it may be either interchangeable or stationary. If your facet head has a stationary index gear, you will need to use a standard circular conversion chart to show you how to convert from the gear you have to the index gear that is needed for a special faceting cut you wish to make. The circular conversion chart can be found in many of the faceting instruction books that are designed to teach you to facet without an instructor.

The master lap is your basic lap and remains on the machine at all times, providing a base for all of your other laps. It must be mounted absolutely level and should be clean to prevent grit dirt and polish from clogging the arbor. The mast lap *must* be running absolutely true; otherwise, the laps will not be running true and it will be impossible to cut the gemstone correctly. The drip

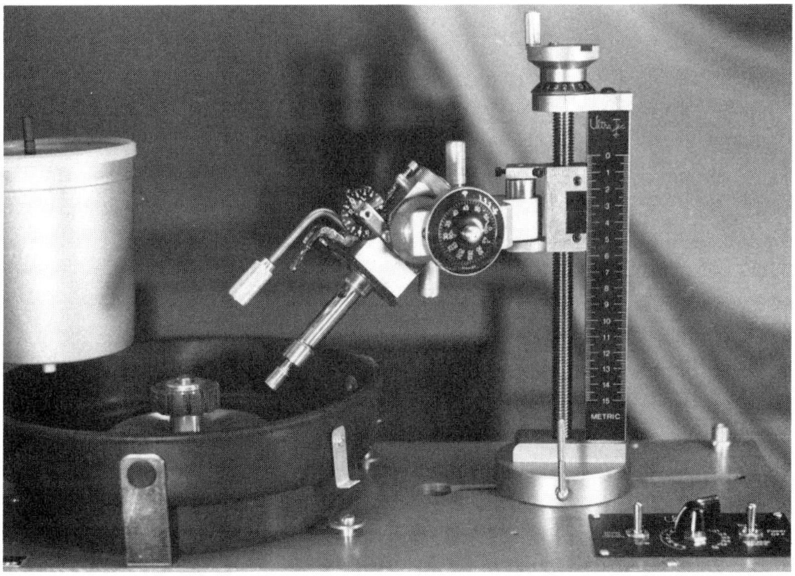

Fig. 11-2 Several types of faceting units now have a sturdy rack-and-pinion stand rod to support the dop arm. Courtesy, Ultra Tec.

pan under the master lap usually has one section in the rim of the pan that is removable so that the pan can be cleaned easily. The master lap is usually either machined aluminum or iron.

Beginning faceters should have at least two cutting laps and two polishing laps, since two polishes should not be mixed on the same side of a polishing lap. If the polishing lap is two-sided, you can use a different polish on each side of the lap, but be careful that you do not contaminate the side not being used. Try to use a separate lap for each polish rather than using a double-sided lap, and always mark the type of polish used in the center of the lap near the arbor hole. If you use diamond polish, mark the grit or micron size in the center. Fine diamond powder grit sizes are difficult to determine once they are applied to the lap. If you use polishing powder, mark the lap with the initial or an abbreviation of the powder, since all white powders, such as tin oxide, levigated alumina, and Linde A, look the same on the lap.

CUTTING LAPS

In the early days of the faceting hobby, diamond-charged laps were expensive and most hobbyists resorted to charging their own laps. Other hobbyists used loose grit or bort on a cast-iron, typemetal, tin-typemetal, or copper lap, or they purchased a double-sided copper lap and charged it themselves, with 400 grit on one side and 600 grit on the other.

In the 1950s, diamond-charged copper laps became popular. Today it is possible to secure a wide range of diamond charged laps in several grit sizes. Lead laps are still available but are rarely used because of the hazards of lead poisoning. Copper laps are still available, as are the solid steel and solid aluminum discs. Steel and aluminum laps are usually precharged and are available in grit sizes of 180, 260, 400, 600, 1,200, and 3,000.

If you cannot obtain a lap in grit sizes 180, 400, or 600, you can buy a copper lap and charge it with the grit size you need. Always mark the grit size on the lap in the center near the arbor hole. Diamond powder or bort is available in a wide range of grit or micron sizes, ranging from 180 grit to 100,000 microns. (Diamond grit sizes beyond 3,000 are usually specified in microns.) Diamond powder can be purchased in a one-carat vial or a five-carat quantity.

Some hobbyists who facet but who have cabochon equipment as well often preform the stone to be faceted on the cabochon grinding wheels. Stones that are 8 or more in hardness should be preformed on the coarse diamond

Fig. 11-3 A complete faceting unit, two grinding laps (one is on the master lap of the machine), two polishing laps, a transfer V-block, a 45° dop, and a set of metal dop sticks. Courtesy, M D R Manufacturing Company.

faceting lap. Many faceters use a 280 grit diamond lap for preforming the stone and then switch to a finer lap for cutting the facets.

POLISHING LAPS

Polishing laps are available in plastic, tin, tin-typemetal, typemetal, and fine diamond-charged tin, as well as wax laps and a recent addition, a ceramic lap. Some laps can be used just as they are for polishing small stones. For larger

FACETING LAP KITS

Two types of faceting lap kits can be purchased. One kit has 8-inch-diameter (20.32 cm) diamond laps in 260 grit and 1,200 grit, plus two 8-inch-diameter (20.32 cm) phenolic laps for polishing. The other kit has 6-inch-diameter (15.24 cm) or 8-inch-diameter (20.32 cm) diamond laps with a 260 grit or 1,200 grit lap. It includes two polishing laps, one a phenolic lap and the other a tin lap.

If you want to build your own faceting desk and mount the faceting head permanently on the desk, there are several suppliers who sell the faceting head separately (see Fig. 11-4).

Fig. 11-4 If you make your own table for faceting, you can buy just the faceting head. Courtesy, M D R Manufacturing Company.

stones, plastic and soft metal laps should be scored. Lucite and tin laps are occasionally prescored by the manufacturer.

Plastic Laps

Of the plastic laps, Lucite and Plexiglas are the best. Plastic laps should be from ½ inch (12.7 mm) to ⅝ inch (15.87 mm) thick. The thinner plastic laps do not hold up well under the heat and pressure that develop when polishing a stone. A plastic lap can accommodate two polishes, using a different one on each side of the lap, but be sure to mark each side with the initials of the polish, and be exceptionally careful not to contaminate the opposite side.

Wax Laps

Wax laps are used only for very soft stones. Some faceting books give instructions for making your own wax laps. Wax laps can be ordered from faceting equipment manufacturers.

Diamond Laps

Most of the precharged diamond polishing laps are charged with 64,000-micron diamond and are designed for polishing stones that are 9 or more in hardness.

Ceramic Laps

Ceramic laps are 8 inches (20.32 cm) in diameter, and one side has been diamond polished to a precision flat surface. They are strictly polishing laps, designed to be used with 50,000 to 100,000 diamond compound. The ceramic lap has a carborundum composition and must be handled with extreme care since the ceramic is brittle and will chip easily. Ceramic laps are good for extremely hard gemstones such as the corundums (ruby and sapphire). Stones under 7 in hardness should be handled carefully.

The lap should be washed in lukewarm water with Lava soap, then rinsed in tepid water. If some of the diamond sticks, it can be removed with a diamond compound thinner.

The recommended speed for a ceramic lap is 50 RPM or less. When working with stones less than 7 in hardness, the stone should be polished on the stationary lap by hand using very little pressure.

Another ceramic lap on the market is designed to be used only on one side. Charging both sides will contaminate the master lap. This lap is charged with graphite and diamond compound (a stick of graphite is furnished with the lap). Only one size of diamond powder should be used on the lap, but the size can range from 14,000 to 100,000 microns with the recommended spray lubricant. Polishing on this lap is done with an up and down movement rather than by the standard movement of polishing across the face of the lap.

DOPPING EQUIPMENT

Besides the faceting unit, you will need an alcohol lamp and either a dopping stove or a dopping pot, as well as a set of dop sticks, which are different from those used for cabochons.

Dop Sticks

Dop sticks for faceting are made of metal, usually aluminum, and the heads are either cone-shaped to hold round, brilliant stones or V-shaped to hold emerald cut, rectangular cut, or square-cut stones.

Most faceting equipment suppliers carry sets or pairs of dop sticks. Purchase a set when you buy the faceting machine so that you can be sure the dop sticks will fit the chuck on the dop arm of the unit. Dops are usually referred to by the size of the head. A set of dops will have one pair of two matching dops of each size. The usual sizes are $\frac{1}{16}$ inch (1.587 mm), $\frac{1}{8}$ inch (3.175 mm), $\frac{3}{16}$

STORING THE LAPS

Each cutting and polishing lap should be kept in a plastic bag to keep it dust-free and stored flat to prevent it from warping. Ziplock storage bags make good covers for your laps. You can buy a cabinet made especially for storing laps or you can make your own. Each lap should have a separate shelf so that they lay perfectly flat. The cabinet should be thick and solid enough so that neither the cabinet nor the shelves will warp. Also, whether homemade or purchased, the cabinet must be placed on a solid and level surface.

---

inch (4.7625 mm), 1/4 inch (6.35 mm), 5/16 inch (7.9375 mm), and 3/8 inch (9.525 mm).

A complete set of dop sticks usually comes with a wooden storage block with holes drilled to fit the shanks of the dop sticks. If a dop-stick set does not have a storage block, you can make your own from a rectangular block of hardwood. Drill six sets of 1/4 inch (6.35 mm) holes to hold the dop-stick pairs opposite each other. Leave enough room between each set of holes so that the dop sticks can be easily taken out, one at a time, without knocking the set over.

V-blocks

You will also need a V-block approximately 4 or 5 inches (10.16 or 12.70 cm) long with aluminum uprights on each end containing a "V" groove to hold the dop stick solidly while transferring the gemstone. The stone and the matching dop must align exactly in order to perfectly align the two dop sticks. The part of the stone that is faceted, usually the crown, can then be aligned and the facets matched with the pavilion facets.

APPENDIX

USEFUL TABLES

Names for Agates, Based on Appearance or Location

algae	amethystine	Apache	Aztec
boquet	Brazilian	Calico	Carey plume
Casa Grande	cathedral	Coyamito	crazy lace
Deming	dendritic	Dryhead	Ellensburg blue
Fairburn	Fairhills	flame	flower
Horse Canyon	iris	jasp-agate	Laguna
Lake Superior	Mexican purple	Moctezuma	Ochoco
oolitic	pigeon blood	polka dot	pompon
Priday plume	Rio Grande	sapphirine	snake skin
Tepee Canyon	Tick Canyon	tube	turritella
Uraguayan	youngite	zebra	

Names for Jaspers

cycad	regalite	tempskya

Scales of Hardness

Degree of Hardness	*Name*	*Moh's Scale*	*Knoop Scale*	*Chemical Composition*	*Origin*
10	Diamond	10	6300	C	Natural and Synthetic
	Silicon Carbide	9.4	2100	SiC	Synthetic
	Aluminum Oxide	9.2	1650	Al_2O_3	Synthetic
9	Corundum	9	1425	Al_20_3	Natural
8	Topaz	8	1250		Natural
7	Quartz	7	750	$Si0_2$	Natural
	Flint	7	750	$Si0_2$	Natural
6	Feldspar	6	560		Natural
5	Apatite	5	350		Natural
4	Fluorite	4	163	CaF_2	Natural
3	Calcite	3	135		Natural
2	Gypsum	2	32		Natural
1	Talc	1			Natural

Courtesy of Mary Warzin. Reprinted from "Lapidary Barrel Tumbling" by Joe Warzin.

Grit-Size Numbering and Grading

Grit Size	*Particles per Linear Inch*	*Approx. Number of Particles to Cover 1 Square Inch*	*Number of Silicon Carbide Grains in One Gram of Powder*
100	147	21,609	—
120	179	32,041	—
150	208	43,264	—
180	294	86,436	—
220	385	148,225	—
240	403	162,409	3,500,000
280	571	326,041	4,800,000
320	781	609,961	9,500,000
400	1,111	1,234,321	40,000,000
500	1,538	2,365,444	250,000,000
600	3,030	9,180,900	440,000,000

Courtesy of Mary Warzin. Reprinted from "Lapidary Barrel Tumbling" by Joe Warzin.

Calculated Critical Angles Based on Refractive Index

R.I.	*C.A.*	*R.I.*	*C.A.*	*R.I.*	*C.A.*	*R.I.*	*C.A.*	*R.I.*	*C.A.*
1.30	50.3	**1.67**	**36.8**	2.04	29.4	**2.41**	**24.5**	2.78	21.1
1.31	49.8	1.68	36.5	2.05	29.2	2.42	24.4	2.79	21.0
1.32	49.3	1.69	36.3	2.06	29.0	2.43	24.3	2.80	20.9
1.33	**48.8**	1.70	36.0	2.07	28.9	2.44	24.2	2.81	20.8
1.34	48.3	1.71	35.8	2.08	28.7	2.45	24.1	2.82	20.8
1.35	47.8	**1.72**	**35.5**	2.09	28.6	2.46	24.0	2.83	20.7
1.36	47.3	1.73	35.3	2.10	28.4	2.47	23.9	2.84	20.6
1.37	46.9	1.74	35.1	2.11	28.3	2.48	23.8	**2.85**	**20.5**
1.38	46.4	1.75	34.8	2.12	28.1	2.49	23.7	2.86	20.5
1.39	46.0	**1.76**	**34.6**	2.13	28.0	2.50	23.6	2.87	20.4
1.40	45.6	1.77	34.4	2.14	27.9	2.51	23.5	2.88	20.3
1.41	45.2	1.78	34.2	2.15	27.7	2.52	23.4	2.89	20.2
1.42	44.8	1.79	34.0	2.16	27.6	2.53	23.3	2.90	20.2
1.43	44.4	1.80	33.7	2.17	27.4	2.54	23.2	2.91	20.1
1.44	**44.0**	1.81	33.5	2.18	27.3	2.55	23.1	2.92	20.0
1.45	43.6	1.82	33.3	2.19	27.2	2.56	23.0	2.93	20.0
1.46	43.2	**1.83**	**33.1**	**2.20**	**27.0**	2.57	22.9	2.94	19.9
1.47	42.9	1.84	32.9	2.21	26.9	2.58	22.8	2.95	19.8
1.48	42.5	1.85	32.7	2.22	26.8	2.59	22.7	2.96	19.7
1.49	42.2	1.86	32.5	2.23	26.6	2.60	22.6	2.97	19.7
1.50	41.8	1.87	32.3	2.24	26.5	2.61	22.5	2.98	19.6
1.51	41.5	1.88	32.1	2.25	26.4	**2.62**	**22.4**	2.99	19.5
1.52	41.1	1.89	31.9	2.26	26.3	2.63	22.3	3.00	19.5
1.53	40.8	1.90	31.8	2.27	26.1	2.64	22.3	3.01	19.4
1.54	**40.5**	1.91	31.6	2.28	26.0	2.65	22.2	3.02	19.3
1.55	40.2	**1.92**	**31.4**	2.29	25.9	2.66	22.1	3.03	19.3
1.56	39.9	1.93	31.2	2.30	25.8	2.67	22.0	3.04	19.2
1.57	**39.6**	1.94	31.0	2.31	25.7	2.68	21.9	3.05	19.1
1.58	39.3	1.95	30.9	2.32	25.5	2.69	21.8	3.06	19.1
1.59	39.0	1.96	30.7	2.33	25.4	2.70	21.7	3.07	19.0
1.60	38.7	1.97	30.5	2.34	25.3	2.71	21.7	3.08	18.9
1.61	38.4	1.98	30.3	2.35	25.2	2.72	21.6	3.09	18.9
1.62	**38.1**	1.99	30.2	2.36	25.1	2.73	21.5	3.10	18.8
1.63	37.8	2.00	30.0	2.37	25.0	2.74	21.4	3.15	18.5
1.64	37.6	2.01	29.8	2.38	24.8	2.75	21.3	3.20	18.2
1.65	37.3	2.02	29.7	2.39	24.7	2.76	21.2	3.25	17.9
1.66	37.0	2.03	29.5	2.40	24.6	2.77	21.2	3.30	17.6

Note: The values set in **bold type** are the most significant values. (These are not the angles of pavilion facets.)
Courtesy of Lapidary Journal, Inc.

Conversion Table

Length

1.61 kilometers	=	1 mile
0.91 meter	=	1 yard
.30 meter	=	1 foot
30 centimeters	=	1 foot
2.54 centimeters	=	1 inch

Temperature

To convert celsius to Fahrenheit, multiply the celsius reading by $\frac{9}{5}$ and add 32 to the result.
To convert Fahrenheit to celsius, subtract 32 from the Fahrenheit reading and multiply by $\frac{5}{9}$.

0°C = 32°F (freezing point)
5°C = 41°F
10°C = 50°F
20°C = 68°F
30°C = 86°F
37°C = 98.6°F (normal body temperature)
40°C = 104°F
50°C = 122°F
60°C = 140°F
70°C = 158°F
80°C = 176°F
90°C = 194°F
100°C = 212°F (boiling point)

Volume

0.76	cubic meter	=	1 cubic yard
0.03	cubic meter	=	1 cubic foot
3.8	liter	=	1 gallon
0.95	liter	=	1 quart
0.47	liter	=	1 pint
0.24	liter	=	1 cup
29.57	cubic centimeters	=	1 fluid ounce
14.78	cubic centimeters	=	1 tablespoon
4.92	cubic centimeters	=	1 teaspoon

Weight

One carat equals 0.200 milligram by international metric standards. (This should not be confused with *karat*, which is a measure of the fineness of gold.

5 carats	=	1 gram
200 milligrams	=	1 carat
1000 grams	=	1 kilogram
28.35 grams	=	1 avoirdupois ounce = 141.75 carats
37.8 grams	=	1 troy ounce
453.6 grams	=	1 avoirdupois pound = 2268 carats
2.203 pounds	=	1 kilogram (1000 grams)
0.05 metric grain	=	1 grain ¼ of a metric carat
1/20 gram = ¼ carat	=	1 pearl grain (*not* the equivalent of the avoirdupois grain)
4 pearl grains	=	1 carat
1/12 pound	=	1 troy ounce (most opal is sold by the troy ounce)

Suggested Diamond Saw Speeds

Diameter	*rpm*
6"	2,500
8"	2,000
10"	1,500
12"	1,200
14"	950
16"	850
20"	800

RPM Speed Table

This table of rpm speeds in relation to pulley sizes that will be useful to all machine operators. The speed of the motor used is 1725 rpm. These pulley sizes shown in centimeters are based on standard direct conversion of 2.54 cm per 1" and do not reflect standardized metric pulley sizes.

Diameter of Motor Pulley in Inches (cm)	*Diameter of Pulley on Machine in Inches (cm)* 1¼ (3.175)	1½ (3.81)	1¾ (4.44)	2 (5.08)	2¼ (5.72)	2½ (6.35)	3 (7.62)	4 (10.16)	5 (12.7)	6½ (16.51)	8 (20.32)	10 (25.4)	12 (30.48)
1¼ (3.175)	1725	1437	1232	1078	958	862	718	539	431	331	269	215	179
1½ (3.81)	2070	1725	1478	1293	1150	1035	862	646	517	398	323	258	215
1¾ (4.44)	2415	2012	1725	1509	1341	1207	1006	754	603	464	377	301	251
2 (5.08)	2760	2300	1971	1725	1533	1380	1150	862	690	530	431	345	287
2¼ (5.72)	3105	2587	2217	1940	1725	1552	1293	970	776	597	485	388	323
2½ (6.35)	3450	2875	2464	2156	1916	1725	1437	1078	862	663	539	431	359
3 (7.62)	4140	3450	2957	2587	2300	2070	1725	1293	1035	796	646	517	431
4 (10.16)	5520	4600	3942	3450	3066	2760	2300	1725	1380	1061	862	690	575
5 (12.7)	6900	5750	4928	4312	3833	3450	2875	2156	1725	1326	1078	862	718
6½ (16.51)	8970	7475	6407	5606	4983	4485	3737	2803	2242	1725	1401	1121	934
8 (20.32)		9200	7885	6900	6133	5520	4600	3450	2760	2123	1725	1380	1150
10 (25.4)			9857	8625	7666	6900	5750	4312	3450	2653	2156	1725	1437
12 (30.48)					9200	8280	6900	5175	4140	3184	2587	2070	1725
15 (38.1)							8625	6468	5175	3980	3234	2587	2156
18 (45.72)								7762	6210	4776	3881	3105	2587

Courtesy of Lapidary Journal.

Speed of Driven Pulley Required

Diameter and speed of driving pulley and diameter of driven pulley are known.

Rule: Multiply the diameter of the driving pulley by its speed in revolutions per minute and divide the product by the diameter of the driven pulley.

Example: If the diameter of the *driving* pulley is 12" and its speed is 1725 revolutions per minute, and the diameter of the driven pulley is 6.5", then the speed of the driven pulley is 12 × 1725 ÷ 6.5 = 3184 revolutions per minute. (This rule and example apply to this chart.)

Diameter of Driven Pulley Required

Diameter and speed of driving pulley and revolutions per minute of driven pulley are known.

Rule: Multiply the diameter of the driving pulley by its speed in revolutions per minute, and divide the product by the required speed of the driven pulley.

Example: If the diameter of the *driving* pulley is 1.5" or 1½" and its speed 1725 revolutions per minute, and the driven pulley is to rotate 862.5 revolutions per minute, then the diameter of the driven pulley is 1.5 × 1725 ÷ 862.5 = 3" diameter pulley.

Diameter of Driving Pulley Required

Diameter and speed of driven pulley, and speed of driving pulley are known.

Rule: Multiply the diameter of the driven pulley by its speed in revolutions per minute, and divide the product by the speed of the driving pulley.

Example: If the diameter of the *driven* pulley is 5" and its required speed, 1035 revolutions per minute, and the speed of the driving pulley is 1725 revolutions per minute, then the diameter of the driving pulley is 5 × 1035 ÷ 1725 = 3" diameter pulley.

GEM AND MINERAL MAGAZINES

The Earth Science Magazine
4220 King Street
Alexandria, Virginia 22302

First published 1946; quarterly. Specializes in all the earth sciences. For amateur collector, geologist, semiprofessional, and professional.

Gems & Gemology
1660 Stewart Street
Santa Monica, California 90404

First published 1934; quarterly. The journal of the Gemological Institute of America. For the professional, graduate, and student gemologist.

The Lapidary Journal Magazine
3564 Kettner Boulevard
P. O. Box 80937
San Diego, California 92138

First published 1946; monthly. Specializes in gem collecting, gem cutting, jewelry, field trips, and gemology. For all hobbyists, novice and advanced, as well as semiprofessional.

The Mineralogical Record
P. O. Box 35565
Tucson, Arizona 85740

First published 1970; bimonthly. Specializes in mineralogy. For the advanced amateur, semiprofessional and professional mineralogists, and mineral collectors.

ROCK & GEM Magazine
2660 East Main Street
Ventura, California 93003

First published 1971; monthly. Specializes in gems, minerals, and field trips. For gem and mineral hobbyists.

Rocks & Minerals
Heldref Publication
4000 Albemarle Street, N.W.
Washington, D. C. 20016

First published 1928; bimonthly. Specializes in minerals, rocks, and fossils. For anyone interested in minerals, rocks, and fossils.

IVORY IMPORTING RESTRICTIONS

Because of the exploitation of ivory-bearing mammals, the Government has strict restrictions concerning the importing of ivory for sale in the United States. Only those importers who have a Federal Importing License can bring ivory into the United States. The conservation of our natural resources has made it imperative that the restrictions be enforced.

California has enacted its own restrictions, which are more stringent than the federal restrictions. The California restrictions were effective June 1, 1977. The federal restrictions were effective June 11, 1978.

REFERENCES

BOOKS

American Geological Institute. *Dictionary of Geological Terms.* Anchor Books, Anchor Press/Doubleday, Garden City, New York, 1974.

Balej, Ronald J. *Tumbler's Guide.* Minnesota Lapidary Supply Corporation, Minneapolis, 1981.

Baxter, William T. *Jewelry, Gem Cutting, and Metalcraft,* With Section on Identification of Gems by Henry C. Dake. McGraw-Hill, New York, 1938.

______. *Jewelry, Gem Cutting, and Metalcraft.* Third edition, revised and enlarged. McGraw-Hill, New York, 1950.

Book of Gem Cuts. MDR Manufacturing Company, Woodland Hills, California. Vols. 1 and 2, 1971. Vol. 3, 1977.

Dake, H. C., Dr. *The Art of Gem Cutting, Complete.* Fourth edition. Mineralogist Publishing Company, Portland, Oregon, 1949.

Dake, H. C., Fleener, Frank L., and Wilson, Ben Hur. *Quartz Family Minerals.* McGraw-Hill, New York, 1938.

Dana, Edward Salisbury, and Ford, William E. *A Textbook of Mineralogy with an Extended Treatise on Crystallography and Physical Mineralogy.* Fourth edition, revised and enlarged. John Wiley & Sons, New York, 1949.

Daniel, G. L. *Tumbling Techniques: A Guide to Tumble Polishing, A Consensus of Findings.* Lowell R. Gordon, Long Beach, California, 1957.

Gump, Richard. *Jade: Stone of Heaven.* Doubleday, Garden City, New York, 1962.

Grigg, Richard W., Ph.D. *Hawaii's Precious Corals.* Island Heritage Limited, 1977.

Hansford, S. Howard. *Chinese Jade Carving.* Lund Humphries, London, 1950.

Hoffman, Douglas L. *Comprehensive Faceting Instructions.* Aurora Lapidary Books, Spokane, Washington, 1968.

Howard, J. Harry. *Revised Lapidary Handbook.* Published by the author, Greenville, South Carolina, 1946.

Huey, Marshall, and Huey, Dorothy. *Rockhounds Pronouncing Dictionary.* Bellevue Gem & Rock Shop, Laureldale, Pennsylvania, 1973.

Hyde, Christopher S., and Matthews, Richard A. *The Complete Book of Rock Tumbling.* Chilton Book Company, Radnor, Pennsylvania, 1977.

Kennedy, Gordon S., et al. *The Fundamentals of Gemstone Carving.* Compiled and edited by Pansy D. Kraus. Lapidary Journal, Inc., San Diego, 1967.

Kunz, George Frederick. *The Curious Lore of Precious Stones.* J. B. Lippincott, Philadelphia, 1913. (Now in paperback.)

Laufer, Berthold. *Jade: A Study in Chinese Archaeology and Religion.* Dover Publications, New York, 1974.

Leiper, Hugh, F.G.A., and Kraus, Pansy D. *Gem Cutting Shop Helps: The Best Selected From 17 Years of The Lapidary Journal.* Lapidary Journal, Inc., San Diego, 1964.

Liddicoat, Richard T., Jr. *Handbook of Gem Identification.* Eleventh edition. Gemological Institute of America, Los Angeles (Santa Monica), 1981.

Liddicoat, Richard T., Jr., and Copeland, Lawrence T. *The Jewelers' Manual.* Second edition. Gemological Institute of America, Los Angeles (Santa Monica), 1970.

Linsley, Leslie. *Scrimshaw: A Traditional Folk Art, A Contemporary Craft.* Hawthorn Books, New York, 1976.

Nott, Stanley Charles. *Chinese Jade Throughout the Ages.* Second edition. Charles E. Tuttle, Rutland, Vermont, 1962.

Parsons, Charles J., G.G., F.G.A. *Practical Gem Knowledge for the Amateur.* The Lapidary Journal, Inc., San Diego, 1972.

Parsons, Charles J., G.G., F.G.A., and Soukup, Edward J., G.G., F.G.A., *Gem Materials Data Book.* Gems & Minerals, Mentone, California, 1957.

______. *A Handbook of Gems and Gemology.* Gembooks, Mentone, California, 1961.

Pough, Frederick H. *A Field Guide to Rocks and Minerals.* Fourth edition. Houghton Mifflin, Boston, 1976.

Quick, Lelande. *The Book of Agates and Other Quartz Gems.* Chilton Book Company, Radnor, 1974.

Quick, Lelande, and Leiper, Hugh. *Gemcraft, How to Cut and Polish Gemstones.* Second edition, revised by Pansy D. Kraus. Chilton Book Company, Radnor, 1977.

Ransom, Jay Ellis. *The Rock-Hunters Range Guide, How and Where to Find Minerals and Gem Stones in the United States.* Harper & Row, New York, 1962.

Rice, Patty G., Ph.D. *The Golden Gem of the Ages.* Van Nostrand Reinhold, New York, 1980.

Ridge, A. V. *Pro-Am Tumble-Grind Tumble-Polish Guide.* A.V.R. Company, 1972.

Shipley, Robert M. *Dictionary of Gems and Gemology.* Sixth edition, revised and updated. Gemological Institute of America, Los Angeles (Santa Monica), 1974.

Sinkankas, John. *Gem Cutting: A Lapidary's Manual.* Second edition. D. Van Nostrand Company, New York, 1962.

Soukup, Edward J. *Facet Cutters Handbook.* Gembooks, Mentone, California, 1968.

Spencer, L. J. *A Key to Precious Stones.* Third edition. Emerson Books, New York, 1971.

Sperisen, Francis J. *The Art of the Lapidary.* Bruce Publishing Company, Milwaukee, 1961.

Streeter, Edwin W. *Precious Stones and Gems.* Third edition. George Bell & Sons, London, 1882.

Victor, Arthur Earl, and Victor, Lila Mae. *Gem Tumbling and Baroque Jewelry Making.* Victor Agate Shop, Spokane, Washington, 1962.

Warzin, Joe. *Lapidary Barrel Tumbling.* Warzin's Rock Shop, Cleveland, Ohio, 1971.

Webster, Robert, F.G.A. *Gems: Their Sources, Descriptions and Identification.* Fourth edition. Revised by B. W. Anderson. Butterworths & Company, London, 1983.

Weinstein, Michael. *The World of Jewel Stones.* Sheridan House, New York, 1958.

Whitlock, Herbert P., and Ehrmann, Martin L. *The Story of Jade.* Sheridan House, New York, 1949.

Willems, Daniel J. *Gem Cutting.* Charles A. Bennett Company, Peoria, Illinois, 1948.

Young, Fred S. *The Art of Gem Cutting Complete.* Second edition. Mineralogist Publishing Company, Portland, Oregon, 1942.

MAGAZINES

Gems & Minerals

"About the AFMS" *The AFMS Newsletter.* July 1982, no. 537, pp. 51–52.

Grundke, William. "The Art of Intarsia." Part 1. December 1981, no. 530, pp. 14–18.

______. "The Art of Intarsia." Part 2. January 1982, no. 531, pp. 54–55.

______. "The Art of Intarsia." Part 3. February 1982, no. 532, pp. 32–33.

______. "The Art of Intarsia." Part 4. March 1982, no. 533, pp. 30–34.

______. "The Art of Intarsia." Part 5. April 1982, no. 534, pp. 20–23.

______. "The Art of Intarsia." Part 6. May 1982, no. 535, pp. 44–47.

______. "The Art of Intarsia." Part 7. June 1982, no. 536, pp. 34–35, 46–47.

Kronberg, Bernard N. "Competitive Freeform Cabochons." August 1982, no. 538, pp. 16–25.

The Lapidary Journal

Allen, Jean. "Idar-Oberstein, Europe's Jewel City." Vol. 34, no. 4, July 1980, pp. 990–92.

Anonymous. "Holy Intarsia in Gemstones." Vol. 13, no. 4, October 1959, pp. 564–66.

______. "Idar-Oberstein." Vol. 16, no. 5, August 1962, p. 494.

Baughman, Carl A. "Lapidary Use of Black Coral." Vol. 35, no. 1, April 1981, pp. 142–44.

Boyajian, William E., G.G. "A GIA Tour to the Gem Centers of Europe." Vol. 36, no. 5, August 1982, pp. 856–70.

Brockett, Bernard O. "Rock Trails in Michigan's Copper Country." Vol. 26, no. 3, June 1972, pp. 490–99.

Carter, Lee. "Footnote on Chlorastrolites." Vol. 23, no. 7, October 1969, pp. 1026–27.

______. "Intarsia Venture." Vol. 28, no. 5, October 1974, pp. 862–64.

Charles, Russell J., G.G., F.G.A. "The Challenge of Carving Coal." Part I. Vol. 23, no. 12, March 1970, pp. 1662–67.
Choate, Sharr. "Gem Intarsia, Rediscovery of a Lost Art." Vol. 17, no. 8, November 1963, pp. 801–4.
Church, Pearl Dee. "Mosaics in Stone." Vol. 16, no. 7, October 1962, pp. 690–92.
Cluett, Jack. "Famous Painting Inspires Carving." Vol. 17, no. 2, May 1963, pp. 278–80.
Cole, Aubrey E. "To Carve a Cat." Vol. 22, no. 3, June 1968, pp. 400-12.
Colhour, Olive M. "The Blooming Coral Tree." Vol. 24, no. 1, April 1970, pp. 64–69.
______. "A Dream Come True." Vol. 23, no. 3, June 1969, pp. 434–35, 438.
______. "El Picaro." Vol. 22, no. 1, April 1968, pp. 118–22.
______. "The Fuschsia." Vol. 24, no. 3, June 1970, pp. 464–71.
______. "Heavenly Light, An Inspiring New Intarsia." Vol. 17, no. 3, June 1963, pp. 340–41.
______. "The Legend of Happy Fellow." Vol. 28, no. 3, June 1974, pp. 502–5.
______. "Lily-of-the-Valley." Vol. 23, no. 7, October 1969, pp. 922–26.
______. "Sir Winston Churchill—Our First Honorary American Citizen, A Unique Situation." Vol. 28, no. 1, April 1974, pp. 60–66.
______. "Tell a Story—Composite Carvings Should Convey a Message." Vol. 29, no. 5, August 1975, pp. 908–13, 929–30.
______. "These Are Mine." Vol. 29, no. 1, April 1975, pp. 32–36, 40.
______. "When I See Red." Vol. 11, no. 5, December 1957, pp. 504–12.
Courter, E. W. "The Chlorastrolite: Now Michigan's Official Gem." Vol. 28, no. 8, November 1974, pp. 1296–1301.
Crain, Tom, and Boulier, Ken. "Working with Ivory." Vol. 35, no. 1, April 1981, pp. 72–73.
Dahlberg, Jean C. "Thomsonite, The Gem with the Scots Name." Vol. 28, no. 1, April 1974, pp. 42–50, 58.
Deane, Neville. " 'Blue John' Fluorite and Whitby Jet." Vol. 14, no. 5, December 1960, pp. 416–17.
Ferguson, Robert W. "Wonderstone, Moss Agate and Mosquitos." Vol. 38, no. 1, April 1984, pp. 84–97.
Freeze, James, Mr. and Mrs. "Two Rockhounds Visit Europe." Vol. 16, no. 10, January 1963, pp. 970–72.
"Gem Fragments Become Art Pictures." Vol. 18, no. 5, August 1964, pp. 596–99.

Giannola, Pearl. "The Story of the 'Marine Life' Intarsia." Vol. 18, no. 12, March 1965, pp. 1268–75.

Greenspan, Jack. "Charoite." Vol. 37, no. 6, September 1983, pp. 868–69.

Hanneman, W. William, Ph.D. "Don't Throw Away Good Saw Coolant." Vol. 30, no. 10, January 1977, p. 2401.

Howard, Margaret Ann. "Magnificent Mosaics." Vol. 28, no. 8, November 1974, pp. 1266–67.

Hubbell, May. "Pictures in Gemstone—From the Ultimate Art to Pictures You Can Do." Vol. 34, no. 11, February 1981, pp. 2364–76.

Jensen, David E. "Gemstone Carvings from Idar-Oberstein." Vol. 23, no. 2, May 1969, pp. 364–65.

Jones, Meredith R. "The Marsh Hawk Intarsia." Vol. 18, no. 7, October 1964, pp. 742–46.

Jones, Robert W. "Fantasy in Quartz." Vol. 29, no. 1, April 1975, pp. 154–58.

Kraus, Pansy D., G.G., F.G.A. "A Visit with the Maui Divers." Vol. 35, no. 1, April 1981, pp. 118–34.

______. "Ivory and Whitby Jet." Vol. 19, no. 5, August 1965, pp. 546–48, 558–59.

Kurtzeman, Jeffrey J. "Iwo Jima, A Memorial in Faceted Quartz: Jerry Muchna Turns His Artistry to Great Moments in America." Vol. 31, no. 2, May 1977, pp. 590–94.

______. "Jerry Muchna Facets 'The Daisy'." Vol. 32, no. 11, February 1979, pp. 2332–34, 2338.

Lilleberg, Linar. "The Desert Sentinel." Vol. 11, no. 6, February 1958, pp. 616–18.

Longnecker, Paul. "The Tuscarora Intarsia." Vol. 30, no. 11, February 1977, pp. 2476–80.

Lundstrum, W. G. "My Trip to Idar-Oberstein." Vol. 5, no. 1, April 1950, pp. 72–75.

Maline, Maury and Opal. "Award Winning Carvings in Full Four-Colors." Vol. 18, no. 3, June 1964, pp. 384–85.

McConnell, Cecil L. "A Procedure for Intarsia." Vol. 22, no. 4, July 1968, pp. 550–51.

Milliken, Ruth. "Mineral and Gem Tour to Spain and Idar-Oberstein." Vol. 27, no. 11, February 1974, pp. 1690–99

Moore, J. B. "Building a Three-Headed Sphere Machine." Vol. 35, no. 5, August 1979, pp. 1108–17.

Muchna, Jerry. "Faceted Novelties." Vol. 25, no. 11, Feb. 1972, pp. 1550–52.

Munz, William. "A Big Saw to Cut Large Jade." Vol. 25, no. 2, May 1971, pp. 402–4.

Musick, Robert M. "Portraits in Shell." Vol. 13, no. 6, February 1960, pp. 728–32.

Nassau, Kurt, Ph. D. "Natural, Treated, and Synthetic Amethyst-Citrine Quartz." Vol. 35, no. 1, April 1981, pp. 52–60.

Payson, Samuel E. "Bird Intarsias Show the Color Range in Stones." Vol. 20, no. 12, March 1967, pp. 1390–92.

Pough, Frederick H., Ph.D. "Colored Synthetic Quartz from Russia." Vol. 24, no. 3, June 1970, pp. 444–46.

______. "A Skyscraper for Idar-Oberstein." Vol. 24, no. 8, November 1970, pp. 1058–60.

Purteet, Bryan and Ida. "Idar-Oberstein, A Trip Through Europe's Oldest Gem Center." Vol. 21, no. 11, February 1968, pp. 1385–87.

Quick, Lelande. "About Our Cover (Lady Yang)." Vol. 4, no. 2, June 1950, p. 124.

______. "The Mosaic Craft of Joseph A. Phetteplace." Vol. 11, no. 4, October 1957, pp. 424–32.

Reban, Jan, M.D. "Moldavite—The Gemmy Tektites." Vol. 38, no. 1, April 1984, pp. 30–32.

"Rockhounds Run Risk of Skin and Nerve Damage." Vol. 30, no. 7, October 1976, p. 1668. (U.S. Environmental Protection Agency.)

Rolf, Almeida, Prof. Dr. "Soapstone Carving in Brazil." Vol. 24, no. 5, August 1970, pp. 744–49.

"Ruth Pitman's Rock Tapestries." Vol. 35, no. 5, August 1981, pp. 1098–99.

Sarofim, E., Dr. "Idar-Oberstein." Vol. 24, no. 5, August 1970, pp. 733–36.

Sassen, Robert. "The Mosaics of Greece and Italy." Vol. 19, no. 4, July 1965, pp. 514–19.

Skidmore, Daisie B. "Mini Minerals to Depict the Earth." Vol. 32, no. 6, September 1978, pp. 1268–76.

Smart, Charles H. "How the Duck Intarsias Were Made." Vol. 17, no. 7, October 1963, pp. 676–88.

Smull, Eve, and Leeson, Shirley. "The Channel Work of Clyde Crossland." Vol. 36, no. 6, September 1982, pp. 1032–38.

Stalling, Laurence. "A Recent Discovery: A 'Gem' of a Friend in Czechoslovakia." Vol. 38, no. 1, April 1984, pp. 32–36.

"A Stone Dealer in Idar-Oberstein." Vol. 24, no. 1, April 1970, pp. 44–45, 48.

Vargas, Glen and Martha. "Ametrine Comes Out of the Dark." Vol. 35, no. 1, April 1981, pp. 270–71.

Wallace, Etta Mae. "The World's Newest and Largest Jade Statue." Vol. 4, no. 2, June 1950, pp. 92–94.

Whepley, Raymond. "The Intarsia Work of Olive M. Colhour." Vol. 13, no. 3, August 1959, pp. 368–74.

Zammit, Paul. "How 'Midday in Algiers' Was Made." Vol. 24, no. 7, October 1970, pp. 916–17.

Zeitner, June Culp. "All-American Gems." Vol. 24, no. 2, May 1970, pp. 300–12.

______. "Amber and Jet." Vol. 35, no. 1, April 1981, pp. 92–99.

______. "Black Can Also Be Beautiful." Vol. 23, no. 1, April 1969, pp. 4–16.

______. "The Challenge of Channel." Vol. 36, no. 1, April 1982, pp. 48–54.

______. "The Gemstone Blues." Vol. 22, no. 4, July 1968, pp. 516–23, 540–41.

______. "The Hing Wa Lee Gallery." Vol. 34, no. 4, July 1980, pp. 880–83.

______. "Lapidary Laureate, Olive Colhour." Vol. 25, no. 5, August 1971, pp. 660–76.

______. "More About Tektites." Vol. 38, no. 1, April 1984, p. 36.

______. "Organic Gems." Vol. 35, no. 1, April 1981, pp. 16–28.

______. "Organic Lapidary Materials at a Glance." Vol. 35, no. 1, April 1981, pp. 240–41.

______. "Pebbles for Palettes." Vol. 26, no. 2, May 1972, pp. 374–82.

______. "Pietra Dura Minatures." Vol. 32, no. 4, July 1978, pp. 884–85, 906–8.

______. "The Softest Lapidary Materials." Vol. 34, no. 6, September 1980, pp. 1236–46.

______. "A State Bird in Stone." Vol. 31, no. 7, October 1977, pp. 1652–53.

SUGGESTED READING

Adair, John. *The Navajo and Pueblo Silversmiths.* University of Oklahoma Press, Norman, 1970.

Agates of North America. The Lapidary Journal, Inc., San Diego, 1979.

Alt, David D., and Hyndman, Donald W. *Roadside Geology of Northern California.* Mountain Press Publishing Company, Missoula, Montana, 1975.

______. *Roadside Geology of the Northern Rockies.* Mountain Press Publishing Company, Missoula, Montana, 1972.

Andrychuk, Dmetro, B.A., M.A., Ph.D. *Gemstone Faceting: The Mathematical Analyses, Calculations Graphical Data For Determining Facet Angles.* Published by the author, Richardson, Texas, 1977.

Balej, Ronald J. *Gem Cutter's Guide.* Minnesota Lapidary Supply, Minneapolis, 1963.

Bancroft, Peter. *Gem & Crystal Treasures.* Western Enterprises/Mineralogical Record, Fallbrook, California, 1984.

Bell, Ed, Bell, Barbara, Bell, Steve, and McQueary, Ralph and Jerry. *Zuni, The Art and the People.* Squaw Bell Traders, Grants, New Mexico. Vols. 1–3, 1975–77.

The Book of Gem Cuts. M.D.R. Manufacturing Company, Woodland Hills, California. Vols. 1 and 2 (1971); vol. 3 (1977).

Branson, Oscar T. *Fetishes and Carvings of the Southwest.* Treasure Chest Publications, Santa Fe, 1976.

______. *Indian Jewelry Making*. Treasure Chest Publications, Tucson. Vol. 1, (1977); vol. 2 (1979).

Bruton, Eric, F.G.A. *Diamonds*. Second edition. N.A.G. Press, London, and Chilton Book Company, Radnor, Pa., 1978.

Choate, Sharr. *Creative Casting*. Edited by Bonnie Cecil De May. Crown Publishers, New York, 1966.

Choate, Sharr, with De May, Bonnie Cecil. *Creative Gold- and Silversmithing*. Crown Publishers, New York, 1970.

Cox, Jack R. *Advanced Cabochon Cutting, Assembled Stones, Special Shapes, Star Stones, Cat's-eyes, Opal*. Gembooks, Mentone, California, 1971.

Chronic, Halka. *Roadside Geology of Colorado*. Mountain Press Publishing Company, Missoula,Montana, 1980.

Cunningham, Lester J. *A Check List of Cabochon Gem Materials and Their Lapidary Features*. Gembooks, Mentone, California, 1963.

Fenton, Carroll Lane, and Fenton, Mildred Adams. *Rocks and Their Stories*. Doubleday, Garden City, New York, 1951.

Gaal, Robert A. P., Ph.D. *The Diamond Dictionary*. The Gemological Institute of America, Santa Monica, California, 1977.

Giacomini, Afton. *Trophy-Winning Facet Cuts*. Gembooks, Mentone, California, 1973.

Gentille, Thomas. *Step-By-Step Jewelry*. Golden Press, New York, by Western Publishing Company, 1968.

Hoffman, Douglas L. *Comprehensive Faceting Instructions*. Aurora Lapidary Books, Clayton, Washington, 1968.

______. *Star Gems*. Aurora Lapidary Books, Clayton, Washington, 1967.

Hunger, Rosa. *The Magic of Amber*. N.A.G. Press, London, (in conjunction with Northwood Publications), 1977.

Hunt, W. Ben. *Indian Silversmithing*. Collier Books, Macmillan, New York and London, 1974.

Jernigan, E. Wesley. *Jewelry of the Prehistoric Southwest*. School of American Research, Santa Fe, and University of New Mexico Press, Albuquerque, 1978.

Jerrard, R. A. *The Amateur Lapidary: A Practical Guide to Cutting and Polishing Semi-precious Stones and Pebbles*. D. Bradford Barton, 1969.

Kennedy, Gordon S., et al. *Fundamentals of Gemstone Carving*. Fourth printing. The Lapidary Journal, Inc., San Diego, 1977.

Klein, James. *Where to Find Gold & Gems in Nevada*. Gem Guide Books, San Gabriel, California, 1983.

Kraus, Edward H., and Slawson, Chester B. *Gems and Gem Materials*. Fifth edition. McGraw-Hill, New York and London, 1947.

Kunz, George Frederick. *Gems and Precious Stones of North America*. Reprint of second edition. Dover Publications, New York, 1968.

Leechman, Frank. *The Opal Book*. Ure Smith, Sydney, Australia, 1961.

Levi-Setti, Ricardo. *Trilobites: a Photographic Atlas*. University of Chicago Press, Chicago, 1975.

Levy, Gordon. *Who's Who in Zuni Jewelry*. Western Arts Publishing Company, Denver, 1980.

Long, Robert, and Steele, Norman. *Facet Design*. Vol. 1, *Ovals*. Second edition. Seattle Faceting Books, Mercer Island, Washington, 1983. Vol. 2, *Navette/Marquise*, 1980. Vol. 3, *Heart & Pear*, 1980. Vol. 4, *Cut Corner Rectangle Emerald*, 1981. Vol. 5, *Rounds*, 1984.

MacFall, Russel P. *Collecting Rocks, Minerals, and Fossils*. Hawthorn Books, New York and London, 1963.

______. "Wyoming Jade." The Lapidary Journal, Inc., San Diego, 1980.

Matlins, Antoinette Leonard, and Bonanno, Antonio C. *The Complete Guide to Buying Gems*. Crown Publishers, New York, 1984.

Michael, Prince of Greece. *Crown Jewels of Europe*. Alexandria Press in collaboration with John Calmann & Cooper, London, and Harper & Row, New York, 1983.

Morton, Philip. *Contemporary Jewelry: A Studio Handbook*. Holt, Rinehart and Winston, New York, 1970.

Mumme, I. A. *The Emerald: Its Occurrence, Discrimination and Valuation*. Mumme Publications, Port Hacking, N.S.W., Australia, 1982.

Nassau, Kurt, Ph.D. *Gems Made by Man*. Chilton Book Company, Radnor, Pa., 1980.

______. *Gemstone Enhancement*. Butterworths, Kent, England, 1984.

Oakeshotte, Peter. *California's Changing Landscapes*. McGraw-Hill, New York, 1971.

O'Keefe, John A. *Tektites and Their Origin*. Elsevier Scientific Publishing Company, New York, 1976.

O'Neil, Paul. *Planet Earth, Gemstones*. Time-Life Books, Alexandria, Virginia, 1983.

Pack, Greta. *Jewelry & Enameling*. D. Van Nostrand, New York, 1951.

Pearl, Richard M. *Cleaning and Preserving Minerals*. Third edition. Earth Science Publishing Company, Colorado Springs, 1971.

Pearson, Bobbie. *Wire Tree Sculpture*. Ronald M. Pearson, Milwaukee, 1982.

Quick, Lelande. *The Book of Agates and Other Quartz Gems*. Chilton Book Company, Radnor, Pa., 1963.

Ratkevich, Ronald Paul. *Dinosaurs of the Southwest*. University of New Mexico Press, Albuquerque, 1976.

Ritchie, Carson I. A. *Scrimshaw*. Sterling Publishing Company, New York, and Saunders of Toronto, Don Mills, Ontario, 1972.

Sherman, Joseph J., Dr. *Angulations: Faceting Step by Step*. Biltmore Press, Franklin, North Carolina, 1976.

______. *Secrets of Creative Gem Stone Cutting (Cabochoning)*. Groves Printing Company, Franklin, North Carolina, 1973.

Sinkankas, John. *Emerald and Other Beryls*. Chilton Book Company, Radnor, Pa., 1981.

______. *Gemstone & Mineral Data Book*. Van Nostrand Reinhold, New York, 1981.

______. *Gemstones of North America*. Vol. 1 (1959); vol. 2 (1976). D. Van Nostrand, New York.

______. *Mineralogy for Amateurs*. D. Van Nostrand, New York, 1964.

______. *Prospecting for Gemstones and Minerals*. Van Nostrand Reinhold, New York, 1961.

______. *Van Nostrand's Standard Catalog of Gems*. D. Van Nostrand, New York, 1968.

Sinotte, Stephen R. *The Fabulous Keokuk Geodes*. Wallace-Homestead Company, Des Moines, Iowa, 1969.

Untracht, Oppi. *Jewelry Concepts and Technology*. Doubleday, Garden City, New York, 1982.

Vanders, Iris, and Kerr, Paul F. *Mineral Recognition*. John Wiley & Sons, New York, 1967.

Vargas, Glenn and Martha. *Descriptions of Gem Materials*. Second edition. Published by the authors, Thermal, California, 1979.

______. *Diagrams for Faceting*. Vol. 1 (1975); vol. 2 (1983). Published by the authors, Thermal, California, 1975.

______. *Faceting for Amateurs*. Second edition. Published by the authors, Thermal, California, 1977.

von Neumann, Robert. *The Design and Creation of Jewelry*. Third edition. Chilton Book Company, Radnor, Pa., 1982.

Walter, Martin. *Gemstone Carving*. Chilton Book Company, Radnor, Pa., 1977.

Watermeyer, Basil. *Diamond Cutting*. Purnell & Sons, London, 1980.

Wiener, Louis. *Handmade Jewelry: A Manual of Techniques*. Third edition. Van Nostrand Reinhold, New York, 1981.

Wright, Ruth V., and Chadbourne, Robert L. *Gems and Minerals of the Bible*. Harper & Row, New York, 1970.

Young, Colonel Brigham. *Gem Trails of Oklahoma*. Alamo Flower Shop, Oklahoma City.

Zeitner, June Culp. *Appalachian Mineral & Gem Trails*. The Lapidary Journal, Inc., San Diego, 1982.

______. *Midwest Gem Trails*. Third edition. Gembooks, Mentone, California, 1964.

INDEX